# Gay Search

# the impatient gardener

garden design consultant
**Bonita Bulaitis**

special photography
**Helen Fickling**

**Quadrille**

Editorial Director: Jane O'Shea
Creative Director: Mary Evans
Art Director: Helen Lewis
Project Editor: Hilary Mandleberg
Art Editor: Rachel Gibson
Production: Nancy Roberts
Picture Research: Nadine Bazar

First published in 2002 by Quadrille Publishing Limited
Alhambra House
27–31 Charing Cross Road
London WC2H 0LS

Cataloguing-in-Publication Data: a catalogue record for this book is
available from the British Library.

ISBN 1 903845 48 3

Printed and bound in Singapore

# contents

instant gratification

# age of the instant

We live in an age of instant everything. We can have what we want almost the moment we decide that we want it. We can prepare a meal in minutes, courtesy of the microwave. We can send a query to the other side of the world and have a reply back in seconds thanks to e-mail. We can track down and buy the out-of-print book we have been after for years in a matter of minutes on the net. We are used to instant gratification and, in the twenty-first century, patience is no longer a virtue. We are an impatient generation, and so we have seen the emergence of a new kind of gardener – *The Impatient Gardener.*

What is more, many of us now buying our first home and acquiring our first garden, grew up in flats and have no direct experience of gardening at all. And since we are impatient, what we want is an instant garden, a room outside that we can use right away just as we use the other rooms in our home. For our parents and grandparents, a garden was primarily the space in which you did gardening – growing vegetables, perhaps, as well as flowers – with sitting out and playing games as secondary activities. But the impatient gardener is not interested in the means, only in the end. We want to enjoy our gardens by relaxing in them, entertaining friends, eating out – not by gardening in them. Though it's only fair to warn you, even at this early stage, that many people who have started out purely to create an outside room, while being not remotely interested in gardening, have found themselves horticulturally hooked.

Taking interior design techniques and ideas outside into the garden has been extremely popular in recent years, with vast numbers of magazine articles and television makeover programmes. It can be very successful, but it is not always a marriage made in heaven and some of the results are just plain hideous. Screaming lime green or bright purple may work well in the house, perhaps, but outside in the garden where the ceiling is the sky and the backdrop, urban or rural, is the landscape, these colours can look out of context and jar horribly. And some interior/exterior ideas are wholly impractical and even a few weeks later will look dreadful. Unbleached calico is a cheap, stylish fabric for inside, but use it as an awning in the garden, and after a few days of rain it is covered in green slime and sagging with the weight of water. Plants, where they feature in these outdoor rooms, are often an afterthought, thrown in without a great deal of consideration or care, which is a real shame because gardens are more than just outside rooms, and it's the plants that make the difference. Even one or two will bring life into the space, something of the natural world, and in a small city yard or town garden that is very important.

What *The Impatient Gardener* sets out to do is offer you the best of both worlds – ideas for attractive, well-designed instant projects that look great the moment they are finished but that are also practical and, where plants are concerned, are underpinned with proper horticulture. Far from falling apart or the plants in them dying after a couple of months, these projects will look better and better every year, because, mixed in with the instant gratification, is a little sneaky long-term planning.

Take, for example, planting a new border *Impatient Gardener* style. Read The Soft Touches and you will see that top of your list should be plants that will give you a really good show in their first season – those we are calling the Fast plants. While you are putting these in, though, you're also planting a few that won't really start to shine for a year or two – the Medium or even Slow plants. But this doesn't matter because you will have the Fast plants to give you pleasure straight away. In a year or two, once these have fulfilled their purpose and have either died or been taken out, your Medium and Slow plants will be there ready to take centre stage, with only the minimum additional input from you. Doing the work once and getting the rewards year after year seems to me like a very good deal.

If you are an impatient gardener, there is a risk that you will want to do landscaping or build garden features right away, before you have thought about the garden as a whole. After a while, when you have seen how you use the garden, you may find that the landscaping or features are in the wrong place or just don't work. Mistakes on that sort of scale are dispiriting and expensive.

So even if you know you won't get around to doing everything for some time, from the very start, do think about the whole space and how you eventually want to use it. You may have a good spatial sense and will be able to come up with a plan yourself. If not, consult a garden designer. Arrange to see several, look at examples of their work and if possible talk to previous clients. It is very important to choose someone you like and who you feel is on your wavelength. What a good designer will do is come up with the garden you would have designed for yourself had you known how to do it. It is up to you whether you commission a plan that includes every single detail from the size of the paving slabs and the plant lists to the colour of the cushions, or whether you go for a much simpler plan that gives the layout and basic structure but leaves you to stamp your own personality on it through the detail.

Once you have a plan, you will be able to execute it as time and money allow, knowing that when it is finally finished you will end up with a garden that works as a whole, not a series of unrelated bits and pieces. And since you will be raring to get started – you are an impatient gardener after all – and can't possibly do everything at once, concentrate on an area that will give you most benefit immediately.

Perhaps that area will be the dull view from the kitchen window that you can transform with a handsome pot, planted or unplanted, or with an object such as an obelisk, placed among whatever planting already exists. You will be surprised at what an enormous difference such a detail can make.

Or it might be the entrance from the house into the garden, where a pergola – hung with instant colourful hanging baskets while the climbing plants are starting to scramble upwards – will divert the eye from the wilderness that lies beyond and create an enclosed area that can serve as an outside dining room. Or it could be a seating area in a west-facing corner. This is an ideal spot for sitting out because it catches the evening sun, and you can always create more seating areas in other parts of the garden at a later stage.

A number of the instant projects involve containers, and for good reason. Firstly, many people do not have access to a proper garden, so they have to grow plants where they can – in a courtyard, perhaps, or on a balcony or roof terrace where containers are the only option. Then there are the impatient gardeners who are also mobile gardeners – at a stage when they are moving house every few years and so don't feel it's worth spending money on plants to leave behind. If they use containers and plant them with the right varieties, they can take their plants with them when they go, and create an instant 'garden-from-garden' in their new home. When they finally decide to put down roots, as it were, so can the plants. The plants can simply be taken out of their containers and planted in the soil.

ABOVE **In an overgrown garden, just placing a simple chair among the plants suggests that the wildness is a deliberate choice.**

PREVIOUS PAGE **Although the trees and climbers in this garden are well established, many of the elements can be instant – the painted walls, the sculptural furniture, and the pots planted with large hostas.**

The final reason for focusing on containers is that they give you enormous flexibility. You can place them anywhere – for example to make a screen that will divert the eye from a particularly unattractive part of the garden beyond, to enclose a seating area, or to add colour, interest and focus on a temporary basis in dull or overgrown borders. That is the key – containers are not permanent features, they can be moved relatively easily and do not compromise your plans for the garden in the longer term. Incidentally, you should always go for the biggest and best containers you can accommodate, even if they are expensive. The money you spend on them is never wasted.

The small projects devised for *The Impatient Gardener* are very quick and easy and are designed for you to do yourself. But as you are an impatient gardener, it is safe to assume that you will not want to carry out any major work yourself since this will take you much longer than employing someone to do it for you. So what I set out to do in The Hard Stuff – walls, floors, features and so on – is give you ideas to help you decide what you want, so that you are able to give a clear brief to the professionals who will be doing the work.

Employing people does not come cheap, of course, but then the time/money equation is something that impatient gardeners understand. Turf is instant, looking good the moment it is laid, but it is also expensive. Grass seed is cheap but slow, taking a week or two to come up and then another month or so before it starts to look like a lawn. When it comes to annuals, you could sow a whole bed for the price of half a dozen packets of seeds. And apart from the cost factor, you can grow a much wider variety of plants from seed. There is also the bonus that many of them will self-sow. This means that although the plants themselves will die in autumn, new plants will grow next year from the seeds they have dropped onto the soil without any intervention from you. Or if you really can't wait the six weeks or so for your seeds to come up and start to flower, you could buy trays of bedding plants from the garden centre at ten or fifteen times the price. The smart impatient garden does a little of both.

At the other end of the scale there is nothing like a few big mature plants for instant impact. When you buy these, what you are paying for is time – the years of growth and the care that has been lavished on the plant. Tree ferns, for instance, grow only about 2.5cm (1in) a year, so it is not surprising that a tree fern about 1m (3ft 3in) high, and therefore about 39 years old, costs as much as it does. Plants like these bring such drama to a garden that, especially in a very small space, one or two are all you need to create an effect and so you could argue, they actually save you money.

Since time is of the essence to the impatient gardener, it can be assumed that you will want to spend as much of it as possible relaxing in the garden, having fun and getting pleasure from looking at it, rather than working in it. So, with that in mind, all the projects are designed to be easy to do and, more important, easy to look after. For example, people often think that putting the whole garden down to lawn is a low-maintenance option. Far from it. In order to look good, grass needs weeding, feeding, mowing twice a week in summer, raking, aerating, scarifying, edging . . . need I go on? For busy people who have other things to do with their lives, the truly low-maintenance option is attractively designed hard landscaping combined with easy-care plants. You might worry that hard landscaping means wall-to-wall cement, but with the right combination of plants and slabs, brick or gravel, the overall effect is far from harsh and will certainly offer year-round appeal.

There are plants that require little maintenance and so are ideal for the impatient gardener, but no plant can survive without a bit of attention. Sometimes – like us – they need water and food. But see Keeping it Going for ways of reducing the amount of time you need to spend on routine maintenance tasks. And you may find, as many people do once they start having relationships with plants, that the required gentle pottering – deadheading and so forth – soon ceases to feel like work and becomes a pleasurable part of the day. In fact, an ideal way to unwind.

But enough theory . . .

OPPOSITE **A carefully arranged collection of pottery jars against a painted wall with just a few stems of pussy willow makes an instant display.**

# choose your style

At this point the chances are you are probably getting impatient – you are an impatient gardener after all – and while reading is all very well, you want to be up and doing. So what follows are some ideas for very simple projects that you could easily do in just a couple of hours, including time spent shopping for the things you will need. Two of the projects can be done at any time of year, though ideally not in winter, while the third is one you can do between early spring and late summer.

These instant projects are not designed just to satisfy your need for instant gratification. They are also a way of helping you decide what style of garden you want eventually. And it's never too early to decide on a style because choice of style affects everything – from the basic layout of the garden, the materials you choose for the boundaries, the hard landscaping, the features, the planting, of course, and right through to the accessories and furniture.

Although there are many different garden styles, it is helpful to divide them broadly into three categories. Firstly, there is the romantic or informal style, best summed up in the traditional English cottage garden. These gardens don't have many straight lines: curves are more popular. The materials will be informal too – old bricks, gravel, randomly laid paving slabs, wood, willow, terracotta – and the planting will be dense and casual, often with plants growing into one another.

Then there is the formal garden, where geometry and symmetry predominate. The lines will be straight and the angles square. Some of the same materials may be used as in a romantic garden – brick, stone slabs, gravel – but they will be laid in a regular pattern. Plants will to some extent be tamed – low clipped box hedges for instance, or prominently featured topiary – but within a rigid framework there is room for some sweet disorder. Although Japanese gardens look nothing like western formal gardens, they too are laid out according to clearly defined rules and the plants are kept firmly under control, to look natural, not to be natural.

Our third category is the modern garden. Here the materials are textural and colourful, such as slate or chippings, or contemporary – metal, concrete or decking, for example. The structure also plays a major part in the overall look of the modern garden. As for the planting, modern gardens can be minimalist with very few plants used in a sculptural way, or they can be densely planted with a modern mixture of grasses and perennials.

BELOW RIGHT  In this modern garden, architecture is dominant and the look minimalist. The furniture takes on a sculptural role, and the planting is confined to the well-shaped trees in the background.

BELOW CENTRE  In this formal garden, geometry dominates and the restrained planting is repeated throughout the space to emphasize the formality. Foliage is more important than flowers.

BELOW  A romantic, informal garden with lawn and abundant mixed borders in which a wide variety of plants in a range of colours grow together in sweet disorder.

# informal magic

## YOU WILL NEED
- 5 x large 'long tom' terracotta pots
- 1 x tin multi-surface garden paint
- 1 x *Astelia chathamica*
- 1 x *Canna* 'Erebus'
- 1 x *Miscanthus sinensis* 'Yakushima Dwarf'
- 2 x *Agapanthus* Headbourne hybrids

## performance in pastels

**A** group of identical pots has as much impact on a dull patio or deck as one very large pot, and in the case of the machine-made terracotta 'long toms' used here and painted a subtle green-blue, can be considerably cheaper. By choosing a variety of different plants and grouping the pots together casually, you create an informal look, while using identical plants and arranging the pots in straight lines would be more formal.

To emphasize the tall slender shape of the pots, we chose tall slender plants. One star is agapanthus, with open heads of rich blue flowers in midsummer on long stems with bright green strap-like leaves. The other is a subtle canna, *Canna* 'Erebus', with elegant blue-green leaves and soft peach flowers in late summer. Both need protecting from frost.

To extend the season of interest there are two foliage plants. The first is an architectural evergreen, *Astelia chathamica*, with silvery sword-like leaves, which will survive the winter in most sheltered town gardens. The second is a grass, a dwarf *Miscanthus*, which produces a fountain of slender green leaves and fluffy plumes of tiny flowers that turn to pale beige seedheads in late summer.

For a show all year round, paint a few more long toms and plant them in autumn with tulips, either pink and purple or pale orange and yellow, and for winter interest, plant hardy cyclamen in shades of pink, magenta or white on top. In early summer, swap these pots for those containing the canna and the agapanthus hybrids.

# formal planters

YOU WILL NEED
• 2 x wooden Versailles tubs, approx 45cm (18in) square
• exterior gloss paint
• gritty compost
• 2 x *Lavandula stoechas*

## lavender's blue

**A**lthough using a pair or two pairs of containers in a symmetrical arrangement automatically lends an air of formality, square Versailles tubs, with their connotations of formal seventeenth-century French gardens, are the obvious choice here. They are often planted with traditional box topiary – lollipops, spirals, pyramids – or other evergreens such as the steel blue *Cupressus arizonica* var. *glabra* or variegated holly trained as standards. More recently, evergreen architectural plants such as spiky cordylines or silvery astelias have become a popular choice and while in spring or summer, half-standard roses or fuchsias look lovely, they lack the year-round appeal of evergreens.

Here we have planted two French lavenders – *Lavandula stoechas* – clipped into cone shapes. Keeping them clipped and formal looking means they don't flower, but that's not a great sacrifice because the leaves are such a bright silver colour, have an appealing soft felt-like texture and, with their serrated edges, are an attractive shape. To compensate for the lack of purple flowers, we chose purple for the Versailles tubs – a more exciting colour than the usual black, white or dark green.

# modern metal

**YOU WILL NEED**
- 2 x triangular metal containers
- black enamel paint suitable for exterior use
- broken bricks or paving slabs
- soil-based compost
- 2 x large *Festuca glauca*

## grasses and black paint

If your taste is modern, and you like clean lines and a minimalist look, choose something simple yet striking, like these evergreen grasses planted in tall black triangular containers. A pair placed asymmetrically adds to the modern effect, but if you have a streak of the traditional about you, you could place them symmetrically either side of a door or bench.

The containers are metal, with holes for drainage drilled through the bottom, and are painted black with an enamel paint suitable for outside use. Since they are so tall and potentially unstable, they are half-filled with bricks to anchor them. This is also a useful anti-theft device if you want to place the containers in your front garden, but do make sure they are in the right place before you start filling them. Once they are full you will not be able to lift them either.

To balance the strong angular lines of the containers, you need striking architectural plants with equally simple lines. Evergreen grasses would work very well – the steel blue *Festuca glauca* that we have used here, with its fine stiff leaves like hedgehog spines, is a good example. The taller and softer *Stipa arundinacea*, with its fountain of bronze-tinged light green leaves and sprays of mist-fine flower heads, would also work well, as would *Carex flagellifera*, which has rich metallic copper-coloured leaves and graceful arching flower heads.

If you have a spot where little or no light penetrates – under the steps down to a basement for example – you could create a modern display without living plants. Choose a stylish container (the choice is wide because there is no need for drainage holes) and fill it with sand to hold in place bamboo canes stained in rich shades, bundles of willow or contorted hazel, either left *au naturel* or sprayed matt white. For an inorganic display, you could use the stainless-steel spirals originally designed as tomato supports.

# common situations, common problems

**O**ne thing all impatient gardeners' gardens have in common is that they are not perfect – otherwise you would have no need to be impatient for change. While every garden is unique, it must be said that there are a number of common types of garden and garden problems to which the same solutions would apply. Some of those are featured here. Look at the examples that most closely resemble your own garden and I hope you will see some suggestions that will work for you.

## shady side passageways

ABOVE **Shade-loving foliage plants bring life to this narrow passage, and the seat gives a purpose to what would otherwise have been dead space.**

OPPOSITE **This curved side passageway has a Japanese feel, with old weathered stepping stones laid in the gravel and bamboo casting interesting shadows on the plain rendered walls of the house.**

**M**any houses have a shady area alongside – a side passageway perhaps, linking the front garden to the back. In many cases, an area like this is used for storage, but it is essentially wasted space, which is a pity because it is often what you look out on from the kitchen or living room windows.

For the impatient gardener a shady passageway is ideal because it can be made to look very stylish, very quickly. Firstly you can make it lighter by painting the walls or fences a very pale colour (see pages 42–45). The floor is likely to be gloomy too, so making that a pale colour either with masonry paint, pale chippings or pale grey decking will appear to increase the amount of light the area gets (see pages 68–69).

If yours is an informal garden, consider putting up simple trellis stained bright colours – the horizontals blue and the verticals yellow for example – and hang from it pots of ferns, which are ideal for shade. Or paint the trellis mauve and blue, and grow shade-tolerant fuchsias, lobelia or tuberous begonias instead.

Along the base of the wall, use deep troughs planted with shade-loving hostas and more ferns. If you want evergreen climbers such as ivy, choose a brightly variegated type such as *Hedera helix* 'Oro di Bogliasco' (syn. *H. h.* 'Goldheart') or *H. h.* 'Glacier'. Plain green would look too gloomy.

For a formal look, use shaped dark green or blue trellis and keep the planting simple. Topiary is ideal – a pair of evergreen box balls, lollipops or spirals in square tubs or simple terracotta pots would look marvellous instantly. (Unfortunately, box blight is a problem in some areas. If yours is affected, try *Lonicera nitida* or small-leaved *Euonymus microphyllus* instead.) Add a few pots of hostas, or alternating pots of mind-your-own-business (*Soleirolia soleirolii*) in light green and dark green or some white busy lizzies and the whole area would look cool and elegant.

For a modern look, paint the walls a strong yet light colour – ochre, pale terracotta or turquoise – and fix shelves to the walls with stainless-steel shop fittings. Use light, bright plastic or metal containers for your plants.

If you paint the floor, you could delineate planting areas with spray-painted curves or zig-zags – easy to do if you draw out the pattern with pencil, then mask around it with newspaper and masking tape. Go for bold planting – huge-leaved hostas, perhaps, and New Guinea hybrid busy lizzies in hot tropical scarlet, orange or magenta. If the area is really shady, plant virtually with painted canes, bundles of lime-washed willow wands or dried flower stems. Done full bloodedly, this can look very effective.

ront gardens, all too often, are a mess, whether they consist of a scrubby patch of grass, some grimy slabs or concrete car parking with perhaps an overflowing dustbin and a few weeds to alleviate the monotony. It's such a shame, not only because the front garden forms any visitor's first impression, but also because you have to look at it every day as you go in and out.

Many modern houses have open-plan front gardens, sometimes with covenants prohibiting boundaries. These gardens often consist of poor quality grass and an often unsuitable tree. Here, lawn is usually impractical. The area is too small and it needs a disproportionate amount of work to make it look good. An easier and more attractive alternative is to remove the lawn and replace it with gravel over weed-suppressing membrane and planting. This works very well with architecture from different periods. If you are worried about cats and gravel use chunky gravel, although the membrane underneath will largely deter cats from scratching in it anyway.

For an informal though not traditional look, go for an oriental-style garden with a large handsome piece of rock, some cobbles and just a few plants artfully placed. A Japanese maple would work very well or, for all-year round interest, an evergreen such as *Arbutus* x *andrachnoides*, with its gnarled stems and cinnamon-coloured peeling bark, or a dwarf pine, has the right look. A group of houseleeks (*Sempervivum*) or mossy saxifrages planted around the rock would be all you need to complete the display.

If you prefer formality, try a simplified knot garden with geometric patterns made from plants and perhaps different coloured gravels or chippings. You could use dwarf box to make a low hedge, if you are prepared to wait a year or two for them to knit together. For a more instant result, use topiary – box balls in a grid, for example, or evergreen grasses such as steel blue *Festuca glauca* or green-and-white *Carex comans* 'Frosted Curls', which are small and neat and ideal for making patterns.

Grasses would be ideal for a modern garden – taller varieties planted informally in sweeps and used with materials such as smoky purple slate paddlestones or finely crushed glass.

A combination of contrasting textured materials is a good solution in a very small front garden, creating strong patterns that look good throughout the year even before any plants are added. Add to the graphic nature with architectural plants such as *Euphorbia characias*, sedums and houseleeks.

The concrete car park type of front garden is perhaps the most challenging because there are few truly instant solutions. One option would be to create patterns using very fine coloured aggregate on top of epoxy tile adhesive, which adds only 6mm (¼in) in height to the existing surface. Mark out the patterns with masking tape, and work with one colour at a time.

Using attractively planted containers to divert the eye is another option. They need to be very large and extremely heavy though – painted oil drums for example, with the base filled with rubble or even bolted to the concrete below, because otherwise they will almost certainly be stolen. Alternatively, create low raised beds with railway sleepers, fill the beds with very gritty compost and plant alpines.

ABOVE **This narrow front garden is nothing more than a path and romantic cottage-style planting. It's ideally suited to the architecture of the house.**

OPPOSITE ABOVE **This minimalist front garden relies for impact on structure and hard materials. Black-stemmed bamboo, tied elegantly back with broad straps, reinforces the Japanese look.**

OPPOSITE INSET **A combination of hard landscaping and planting is far less work than lawn for a front garden and looks much more interesting, too.**

# balconies and roof terraces

**W**hen you have no proper garden, any outdoor space you do have is particularly valuable. For the impatient gardener, balconies and roof terraces are ideal because space is limited and so it is easy to make a big difference right away.

If you are planning a roof garden it is essential to consult a structural engineer to check the building's load-bearing capacity first. This will affect the choice of flooring material, of containers and of the compost. Balconies are designed to be load-bearing to some extent, so while you do not need to consult a structural engineer, you do need to give some consideration to weight. Thin ceramic tiles might be a better bet than 10cm (4in) thick limestone.

Decking is a good choice – loose-laid decking squares work well in a small space and are also portable – as are lightweight tiles or rubber made for

outside use. You can even have lawn on a roof, a very 'green' solution. But it needs to be installed by a specialist and the problems of a lawn on a roof or balcony are the same as with small lawns of all kinds. In addition, where do you store a lawn mower if you live on the fifteenth floor?

There are other practical considerations that will also affect the look of the space. The higher you are, the more you are exposed to the wind in particular. You need to create shelter, something that will filter the wind, like trellis or split-reed screening fixed to uprights and attached to the surrounding walls, rather than solid screening, which is liable to get blown down. If you do want something more substantial, like glass, then use panels of toughened safety glass with spaces in between to allow the wind to pass through. But bear in mind that it will need regular cleaning.

OPPOSITE **Open,** informal trellis provides a filter to protect the planting from the wind, but still allows in enough light so the balcony does not feel claustrophobic.

LEFT **A** very narrow balcony becomes invaluable outside living space. Repeating the planting along its length makes it feel more spacious and less cluttered.

BELOW **This** opaque polycarbonate screen offers shelter from the wind and privacy without blocking out the light. The largely evergreen planting means this roof terrace is attractive to look at and, weather permitting, to sit on all year round.

Polycarbonate sheeting is another option. It is translucent rather than transparent, which gives you privacy with little loss of light. Stretched canvas, laced with rope and tied to uprights, is another option, and would give the roof garden a nautical air, though in a wet climate, a man-made fabric, which will not rot, is a better solution.

As for planting, you can build raised beds if the structure will bear the weight of all that soil, or you can grow all the plants in containers. Choose lightweight materials like metal, fibreglass or plastic. Compost should be as light as possible – use either a soil-less type or a mixture of soil-based and soil-less for permanent planting. You could even use extruded clay granules, although you will need to feed the plants regularly – every week or so – as the granules contain no nutrients.

As for plants, you need those that will stand up to conditions that are both windier and hotter than at ground level. Go for plants with a twiggy open habit and small tough leaves – dwarf pine (*Pinus mugo*), potentilla, shrubby honeysuckle (*Lonicera nitida*) – so that the wind can whistle straight through, or plants that bend easily with the wind – bamboos, for instance, and ornamental grasses. Drought-tolerant plants are also a good choice since the wind can have a very drying effect on the compost and on the plant itself. Avoid plants with large thin leaves that can be torn or scorched by the wind, as well as those with tall stiff flower spikes, which will snap rather than bend.

As for furniture, since storing it will be a problem, choose either items that can stay out all year, or those that can fold flat for storage or be used indoors in the winter months.

If you live in a town or city, you probably only have a very small back yard, so it's all the more important to make the best possible use of the space. It will not only give you somewhere to sit when the weather is good, but also something attractive to look at through your windows. And remember that, in many ways, a small back yard is the ideal spot for the impatient gardener. As it's so small, it's possible to make a dramatic difference very quickly.

In such a tiny space, the walls (or fences) will be dominant. If you're surrounded by walls, they might be made of brick, breeze block or render, or even a mixture – a brick house wall for example, adjoining a rendered breeze block wall. Or perhaps your city yard is hemmed in by fencing.

In the long term – if you're staying long term that is – you may well have to replace the lot. But this is expensive and time-consuming, and it could be something you can put off for a year or two.

Meanwhile, if your walls are unattractive, dirty and discoloured, a really quick fix is to paint them a striking colour. If that is too radical for your taste, then try painting just one part of the wall – a corner for example, or a band in the middle of one wall.

Alternatively, painted panels attached to the wall or fence might be a better solution. You could use panels of Perspex, painted with transparent glass paint in glowing jewel colours, so that the texture of the walls behind shows through. This unusual idea will give a lovely light, airy look, which is often just what is needed to give a dingy corner a lift.

Another possibility is to use panels of marine ply painted with a weather-resistant paint. These will give a completely uniform surface.

BELOW **Decking, chunky wooden screening and large plants in pots transformed this small city yard in just a few days. Since the furniture will be dominant in such a small space, it should be attractive as well as functional.**

## small city yards

# city drama

**YOU WILL NEED**

- 2 x panels marine plywood, dimensions to suit the site
- exterior wood paint or stain
- screws, wallplugs and wood filler
- 1 x large metal container 45cm (18in) in diameter
- 1 x *Dicksonia antarctica*
- pebbles in assorted sizes
- 6 x church candles in assorted sizes

## paint the walls • be bold with plants

Our small city yard was 2.2 x 4m (7 x 13ft), with old, discoloured walls that were very dominant. To add instant, dramatic impact, we decided to cover them with panels of marine ply, each painted, with a hint of Mark Rothko, in a different shade of blue – one a strong blue with overtones of petrol, the other a paler, almost lavender shade. Blue is is a cool, relaxing colour and, since it is a component of green, it makes an excellent background for any sort of foliage.

In such a small space, all you need is one big dramatic plant. For interest all year round choose an evergreen: a tree fern (*Dicksonia antarctica*), with its long filigree fronds, is ideal. It's not hardy everywhere, but should survive the winter in a sheltered city yard.

Another attractive option is the Chusan palm (*Trachycarpus fortunei*), with its large architectural, fan-like leaves. Although it looks exotic, it is very hardy. Other suitable alternatives include *Fatsia japonica*, which has evergreen, large glossy, hand-shaped leaves and creamy flowers in autumn; dramatic black-stemmed bamboo (*Phyllostachys nigra*); or the bold *Phormium tenax*, with its upright blue-green leaves and tall stems of dull red flowers in summer.

Any of these plants will grow happily in a container, which is a plus point since your small city yard is very likely to be paved. When you choose your container, make sure it is in proportion to the size of the plant and is equally striking, since the two together will be the focus of attention.

For our project we chose a shiny, round aluminium pot, 60 x 45cm (24in x 18in) whose reflective surface bounces light around – a bonus in such a dark corner. A container in any clean, simple shape in almost any material would work just as well. If you wanted to use a square tub, for example, you could place it diagonally to fit neatly into the corner.

We laid groups of large smooth pebbles around the pot to add interest and to help disguise the rather dull grey paving. We also laid small pebbles over the compost in the container, not only for decoration but to help conserve moisture. As an attractive alternative to pebbles, you could group seashells around the pot or pieces of driftwood.

As a finishing touch we added some chunky, cream-coloured church candles. In the evening, when these are lit, the dancing flames are reflected in the shiny aluminium surface of the container, bringing movement and warmth to the area, and casting shadows of the leaves on the walls. For a more permanent arrangement, you could install outside lighting with an uplighter under the plant to create shadows.

LEFT This carefully sited urn immediately creates a focal point in an overgrown area and prevents the eye from registering the wilderness beyond.

RIGHT A path mown through rough grass instantly changes the nature of the space from 'neglected' to 'intentionally wild'.

## overgrown back gardens

If you move into an older property in need of work, the chances are that the garden will be similarly neglected. It could be a near-jungle or, more likely, a garden that has become just a little overgrown and is really rather dull, with no focus. While your priority will be getting the house straight, you will also want to get some enjoyment from the garden as soon as you can. This means concentrating on a few areas first, with some instant solutions, some of them temporary, which won't compromise the garden you will get around to creating eventually.

Initially, concentrate on the area closest to the house. If you are not sure where to site or how to construct the patio yet, clear the ground, firm it as much as possible, then lay a weed-proof membrane and spread a thin layer of gravel on top. Add some garden furniture, an umbrella and a few large planted containers and you will have a pleasant if temporary place for sitting – a clearing in the jungle if you like.

It is never a good idea simply to rip out an old garden right away. What it has is structure and that is a valuable asset. Large mature plants also act as screens, blocking out unattractive views perhaps and giving you privacy. If some big old shrubs are taking up too much room, try 'standardizing' them – removing the lower branches so that you are left with a bare trunk and growth at the top, like a tree, and more space below.

In the short term, mow the grass if there is any. It may look even worse the first few times you cut it, but if you persevere it will quite quickly start to look better. Trimming the edges makes a big difference, too. The garden immediately looks cared for, and the wilderness beyond appears to be a deliberate choice.

For a more dramatic effect, cut the grass into a strong formal shape – a circle, oval, diamond or even a square. This immediately gives the garden a focus and a sense of order. Mark out possible shapes with hose or biodegradable marking spray, and check how it looks from the upstairs and downstairs windows of the house. If it looks right, then it is right. It is far better to let the shape of the lawn dictate the shape of the beds around it rather than the other way round. Many people plan the beds first, and they wind up with an amoeba-shaped lawn that never looks quite right.

Containers are invaluable in an overgrown garden. A large pot, densely planted and placed in a border, draws the eye. Or use a series of pots, planted with the same colour scheme and placed throughout the garden. The repetition creates a rhythm that carries your eye through and past the neglected areas. Add height with obelisks set in pots and covered in annual climbers such as morning glory, canary creeper or nasturtiums. Or just place a large simple unplanted pot in a border. Introducing an artefact into the wildness makes the garden seem thought about, and cared for.

# suspended animation

## YOU WILL NEED FOR EACH BASKET

- 1 x *Artemisia vulgaris* 'Oriental Limelight'
- 3 x *Lysimachia nummularia* 'Aurea'
- 3 x *Lysimachia congestifolia* 'Outback Sunset'®
- 3 x *Bidens ferulifolia*
- 5 x *Zinnia* 'Profusion Orange'
- 10 x *Tropaeolum majus* 'Tip Top Apricot'
- I x 35-cm (14-in) plastic-coated wire basket
- soil-less compost mixed with water-retaining gel crystals and controlled-release fertiliser

## tumbling nasturtiums

If you have an old tree in your garden, one very quick and easy way of brightening up the whole area is to suspend several hanging baskets from the branches, like large exotic fruits. For maximum impact, make the baskets identical and keep to a limited colour range and, since the baskets will be in dappled shade under the canopy of the tree, choose plants that can cope with those conditions.

Our colour scheme was orange and yellow. To trail down, we used golden creeping jenny (*Lysimachia nummularia* 'Aurea') which not only has golden foliage, but small buttercup-like yellow flowers the length of its long stems. The other *Lysimachia* we used was *L. congestifolia* 'Outback Sunset®, which is bushier, with larger flowers, golden yellow flushed with orange at the base. *Bidens*, with its fern-like foliage and yellow daisy flowers, is another good trailer, and while it flowers more freely in sun, it gives a good enough show in dappled shape. The same is true of zinnias. The one we used was *Zinnia* 'Profusion Orange'. Nasturtiums come in a range of single colours, like *Tropaeolum majus* 'Tip Top Apricot', as well as mixtures, and are happy in shade. As well as planting the baskets with small nasturtium plants, push ten or so seeds into the compost at the same time. These will start flowering later in the summer and will help keep the whole glorious display going for longer.

At the centre of the basket we used a foliage plant, *Artemisia vulgaris* 'Oriental Limelight', chosen for its variegated green and lime-green foliage. In a sunnier position, the variegation would be more gold than lime.

The secret of spectacular hanging baskets is to use as large a basket as possible – these are 35-cm (14-in) plastic-covered wire baskets – and to cram them absolutely full of plants. We used 25 plants in each of our baskets.

The other secret of success is copious feeding and watering. The simplest way to feed the plants is to put controlled-release fertilizer plugs in the compost as you fill the baskets. These release nutrients over a number of months so you do not need to think about feeding again. As for watering, adding water-retaining gel crystals to the compost helps prevent the baskets drying out too quickly. These crystals swell up and hold many times their own volume in water, which is slowly released as the compost dries, but in very hot weather, the baskets will still need watering twice a day. A lance fitting on the hose makes this job very quick and easy.

## virgin plots

virgin plot, start close to
the house and create a
sitting area. Well chosen
furniture and large plants
in containers give it an
established look
immediately.

If you have moved into a brand new house, you will be confronted with a virgin plot – turf, possibly, or just mud – which is likely to be very small, possibly rectangular, often square or, more difficult than either, broader than it is long.

Although you are an impatient gardener, and want to get started on at least some of the garden right away, it makes sense to have an overall plan to which you can work as time and funds allow. Unless you have a strong visual and spatial sense, consider employing a garden designer. In small spaces, one strong idea is often all you need and that is exactly what a good designer will give you.

If you can afford to have the hard landscaping done right away, then do so, because the effect will be instant. If you do not want the whole garden paved, you should at least allow for a decent-sized patio. If you plan to eat on it, for instance, make it the size of a dining room, otherwise the space will feel cramped and uncomfortable.

In a small square garden, consider a triangular- or quadrant-shaped patio. This gives plenty of depth for a table and chairs and also swings the main axis of the garden to the diagonal, which makes the space appear larger. Reinforce this effect by creating a focal point in that far corner – either with a structure of some kind or with phased planting.

Boundaries are another priority (see pages 38–41). The builder may have put up fences or you may have just one fence panel right next to the house on each side of the garden and then a strand of wire to mark the rest of each boundary, or wire may be all you have. If you are having the work done, bear in mind that all boundaries are virtually instant.

If you are planning to have brick walls in three or four years' time when funds allow, you could use

something like wired split-reed fencing, which will last a few years, as a short-term solution. But it will still need to be supported by firmly installed posts, so unless you plan to do the work yourself, there will not be a huge difference in cost between having this or more permanent fencing erected.

As for planting, concentrate on just a few areas to start with – ideally those that are most visible from the house. Include a few Fast plants for an instant display as well as some Medium plants – climbers such as clematis and shrubs – which will come into their own next year and the year after (see pages 126–141).

If money is really tight, you can make a very attractive small garden in one season by sowing seeds of easy hardy annuals straight into the soil. Work out a simple ground plan and for the hard area use gravel over membrane. A '9' shape works well in square gardens, with the tail as the path and the circle as a

seating area, while a '9' elongated lengthways would suit a rectangular plot. In a garden that is broader than it is long, a '9' stretched widthways would be very effective, as would a pair of diamonds side by side since they keep the focus in the fore- and mid-ground, preventing the eye from whizzing straight to the back fence and registering how close it is.

In the resulting borders sow hardy annuals, which will flower where they are sown, in generous informal drifts for impact and in colours that blend into each other. For structure, add a few large pots, planted or unplanted, to the beds, and perhaps an obelisk or two, painted the same colour as the fences. In the autumn, all the plants will die. If you like the arrangement and feel that it works for you, recreate the design with permanent hard landscaping and planting next year, though you will find that many of the annuals have self-sown and will come up again.

ABOVE **Without the beautiful empty terracotta pot placed in the border, this display of small spring-flowering bulbs would not have as much impact.**

# quick ideas for seasonal cheer

**A**s an impatient gardener, you want to start getting pleasure from your garden right away, as soon as you move in and regardless of the time of year. While obviously there is a lot more gardening work you can do in spring than you can in the depths of winter, none the less, there is work you can do even in winter to give you an instant show. And in many ways, it's in the depths of winter that you really need something bright and beautiful to lift your spirits.

Since it is far better to have a master plan before you start making extensive – and expensive – changes to the garden, these are all low-cost ideas that will not compromise any long-term plans for the garden.

The secret of success in whatever you do and at whatever time of year is to be bold. It's no good putting in a few of anything. Don't plant ten narcissi dotted about. Plant 50 and plant them all together! Sticking to just one colour is far more effective than using mixed colours. For maximum enjoyment, choose a position from where you will you see the display most often – from the kitchen window perhaps, or the patio doors.

If you move house in the autumn, choose a prominent bare spot in a border and dig it over carefully, removing any dormant bulbs you come across and planting them somewhere else. Before you plant for winter colour, whether from flowers, foliage or bark, it is a good idea to put some dwarf bulbs – narcissi, irises, scillas – underneath. This will only take you an extra ten minutes or so, and will give you weeks of additional pleasure in the spring.

Bulbs need to be planted at three times their own depth, so the bigger the bulb the deeper the planting hole needs to be. For the best display, set the bulbs out so they are close but not touching, fill in the hole with soil and then put in the plants. Hardy cyclamen, with their striking silver-patterned leaves and small red, magenta pink or white flowers, are a good choice with rich blue scillas, *Iris reticulata* or *Crocus chrysanthus* 'Blue Pearl' or *C. c.* 'Snowbunting' to come up through them in spring. Winter-flowering pansies are another good choice – perhaps warm orange or deep blue with dwarf narcissi such as the early 'February Gold'.

In late autumn/early winter, there's still time to plant tulips. Rich yellow single, double or glamorous lily-flowered tulips look marvellous rising out of winter-flowering pale blue pansies or forget-me-nots.

In winter, when the ground may be frozen or waterlogged and so planting in the soil is not possible, containers come into their own on the patio and in the borders. A mass of pale green-and-white ornamental cabbages would bring lightness on a gloomy day, as would the brightly variegated evergreen *Euonymus fortunei* 'Emerald 'n' Gold'. For maximum impact, plant three in a large pot. If you want to use them somewhere else in the long term, plant them in their plastic pots. They will come to no harm since they do not grow in winter anyway.

Decorative objects can be invaluable in winter, for instance a large empty pot, a wooden or metal obelisk, a handsome piece of garden furniture. Much better to enjoy these now rather than leave them in the garage until you decide where they will ultimately go.

LEFT Spring-flowering bulbs are an inexpensive way to brighten up an area of rough grass.

# lasting pleasure, minimal effort

**YOU WILL NEED**
- 24 x *Tulipa* 'Marmasa' or any yellow tulip
- cloves of garlic
- 18 x rich blue *Viola* x *wittrockiana*
- 12 x blue *Myosotis*

## winter and spring colour

This project is ideal for the impatient gardener. As well as giving instant gratification in the winter, for a small amount of extra work, you will have a display in spring and early summer as well.

Choose a spot that you will see a lot of from the house because you are unlikely to spend a great deal of time outside in the winter and early spring.

Clear the area. Its size is relatively unimportant, but for impact, it needs to be at least 60 x 30cm (2 x 1ft). Plant a minimum of a dozen tulips per 30cm (1ft) square, each tulip evenly spaced and not touching the next and in a hole at least three times its own depth. The deeper the hole, the more likely the tulips are to survive from year to year. If your soil is heavy clay, spread a thick layer of coarse grit or gravel in the bottom of the planting hole. This will improve drainage and help ensure that the bulbs do not rot.

If you have squirrels in your garden, try planting cloves of garlic among the tulips. Squirrels do not eat alliums, which are members of the same family as garlic, presumably because they are put off by the onion smell. This garden has major squirrel problems but the garlic trick seems to have worked because every single tulip came up. If you find the garlic sprouting too, just pull it out!

Fill in around the bulbs with soil, and then plant winter-flowering pansies on top. For greatest impact, go for a single colour and plant them reasonably close together. Don't worry about leaving room for the tulips – they will find space to push up through the pansies. As long as there is some sunlight, the pansies should flower right through the winter and into the spring. Depending on conditions, they should still be going strong when the tulips flower. In case they are past their best then, boost the display with forget-me-nots and you may be lucky, as we were, to find all three flowering simultaneously at some point.

## summer colour

ABOVE LEFT **Easy-to-grow hardy annuals like field poppies and pot marigolds sown direct in the ground give a colourful show all summer long. The bright blue painted picket fence gives a modern twist to cottage-garden style.**

ABOVE RIGHT **Massed containers of bedding plants such as petunias and lobelia have greater impact if they are all shades of the same colour.**

OPPOSITE **Light and airy sweet peas scramble up a wrought-iron obelisk. Pick the flowers regularly to ensure a succession of blooms throughout the summer.**

If you move in spring or summer, the possibilities for instant temporary delight are almost endless. For a start, it's the perfect time to sow seeds either in existing borders – you'll have a good idea by now what is already there – or in bare ground. Hardy annuals really couldn't be easier, and if you stick to the 'bold is beautiful' rule, just a few packets of one or two types of seeds sown now will give you a terrific display. Love-in-a-mist (*Nigella damascena* 'Miss Jekyll'), for example, with its rich blue flowers, bright green feathery foliage and very striking pale biscuit-coloured seed pods is an excellent choice, either grown on its own or with its white cousin, *N. d.* 'Miss Jekyll White'. So are field poppies (*Papaver rhoes*) – a mix like 'Mother of Pearl' with its unusual combination of dusty reds, pinks, peach, lavender and pearl-grey looks quite stunning grown *en masse*.

Sown in late March or early April, most hardy annuals will germinate within a couple of weeks, and can be in flower in as little as five or six weeks. But I know you are an impatient gardener, so for some instant gratification, why not make a simple wigwam, using copper piping rather than canes, tied together at the top with a leather thong or strong jute string. The moment it is finished it makes a dramatic focal point in the border even before you plant annual climbers to scramble up it. Around the base, sow seed of California poppies (*Eschscholzia californica*) in bright orange, a yellow and orange mix or softer pink for a gentler effect. These have very attractive blue-green fern-like leaves and a succession of papery flowers all through the summer. If you want a blue colour scheme, try *Nemophila* or dwarf cornflowers.

Once all danger of frost is past, plant rich blue morning glories (*Ipomoea tricolor* 'Heavenly Blue'),

bought as young plants from the garden centre, at the base of each leg and encourage them to latch on. By midsummer they should be producing a succession of lovely trumpet flowers, each one lasting only for a morning – hence the plant's common name – but produced in such profusion that it doesn't matter. Another less well-known exotic climber is *Ipomoea lobata* (formerly *Mina lobata*), which has sprays of flowers in orange, yellow and cream on the plant all at the same time.

Another means of providing instant gratification while you are waiting for your hardy annuals to come good would be to place a large pot among them, planted with bright spring bedding – forget-me-nots, pink and white daisies (*Bellis*) or wallflowers.

For additional height and impact, place a wigwam or obelisk on a pot, and for spring and early summer colour, plant a small-flowered clematis such as *Clematis alpina* or *C. macropetala*. Grow it in the pot for an instant display now, then, when it is completely dormant in late autumn, you can carefully remove it and plant it out in the garden.

In early summer, when the garden centres are full of bedding plants, achieving instant gratification could not be easier. Again, be bold with your choice. Big groups of the same plant look wonderful. Yes, this is an expensive way to garden but, as we know, 'instant' does not usually mean 'cheap'. As well as the usual suspects – busy lizzies, petunias, stocks, marigolds, osteospermums – look out for some annuals that will give you height. A forest of tall sunflowers, for instance – either the wine-red *Helianthus* 'Claret' or the pale yellow *H.* 'Moonwalker' – would look fantastic, as would a mass of the huge white tobacco plant (*Nicotiana sylvestris*), which is wonderfully scented at night.

the hard stuff

# ways with walls
# and fences

**W**alls and fences are very important to any garden, but they are of particular importance to the impatient gardener because, unlike the soft elements in the garden, they provide instant impact. In smaller gardens they are probably the most dominant element, certainly in the early stages and also in the winter months when there is little to soften, complement or distract from them. For that reason, whether you have existing boundaries, or whether you will have to put them up yourself, it is extremely important that they are not merely functional, but that they are features in their own right.

Boundaries fulfil a number of important functions in the garden, which largely dictate their form. At their most basic, they mark the extent of your property, but if that were their only purpose, a strand of wire stretched between posts – still favoured by developers on new housing estates – would serve well enough. For security, to keep out unwanted visitors, animal and human, and to keep in children and pets, though, more solid boundaries are needed. They are also needed to provide shelter from the elements, to create a warmer microclimate in cold areas, to provide some shade in hotter climates, and protection from the wind both for you and for the plants.

Boundaries are also essential for privacy. For the vast majority of us who live in towns and cities, surrounded on all sides by other people, noise and activity, the need to create a sense of enclosure, a private haven into which we can retreat, is very strong indeed. In this situation the boundaries are both actual and psychological. A picket fence, trellis, a group of shrubs or even a deciduous hedge in winter are by no means solid screens, but behind them we feel enclosed, private, safe.

Boundaries can screen out the rest of the world, hiding unattractive views such as ugly buildings and the furniture of public utilities, but they can also reach out and draw more attractive surroundings into the garden, making a small space appear larger. A densely planted wall or fence can make the boundaries themselves disappear, so that a lovely view, a nearby church spire or even the trees in neighbouring gardens, appear to be part of your garden. The Japanese have a word for it – *shakkei*, meaning 'borrowed scenery' – and it's something that features in many traditional Japanese gardens.

Boundaries can be soft – as in hedges – as well as hard – as in walls and fences – but for the impatient gardener the latter are a much better option because they are virtually instant. In a small garden, a bricklayer could build walls in a week whereas even the fastest growing hedge will take several years to make a decent screen. If you inherit hedges, though, that are functional but little else, there are a number of things you can do to brighten them up very quickly, which we'll come to later in this section.

When you are thinking about boundaries, there are a number of important points to bear in mind. First of all there is scale. The higher the boundary, the smaller it will make the space appear. If you have a small city yard or suburban strip, high walls or fences will make your garden feel like a box or a canyon. Rather than feeling enclosed you may well feel imprisoned. In situations like these, a lower solid boundary with a pierced screen or trellis on top, or even all stout trellis, will create a boundary that feels secure, and, when you grow climbing plants up it, private. Since you can glimpse the sky through it, it does not feel claustrophobic.

High boundaries around small spaces also create a lot of shade, and while some may be welcome, few people want a garden that is shady all the time.

The boundaries will also go a long way to determining the style of your garden. Attractive old brick walls call out for a traditional style of planting, either romantic and

informal – herbaceous borders or the cottage garden look – or architectural and formal, as in parterres. Smooth, rendered surfaces or painted wood suggest something more modern. And boundaries are also crucial in setting the mood – cool and sophisticated perhaps or funky or folksy. They should also take account of the wider setting. Country gardens, for example, look best with informal screens – mixed hedges, perhaps, ideally thorny to make them stock-proof, or on a smaller scale, wattle or willow hurdles or, for the front garden, low picket fences. City gardens, on the other hand, need to reflect the built environment, with walls, smooth-planed rather than rough-sawn fences, cast-iron railings or clipped formal hedges. Suburban gardens need a style somewhere between the two – not too formal but not too informal either.

The choice of materials for boundaries is very important, too, especially in a small space, where you will be close to them and aware of them all the time just as you are of the colours and textures of the walls in a room. In larger gardens, it may be possible to have several different styles of boundary – walls close to the house perhaps, hedges further away – but in a small space, uniformity is the ideal in terms of design because it is less fussy and distracting and makes the space appear larger. If you have inherited boundaries that are a mixture of materials – something that often happens since at least one of your boundaries will be owned by your neighbours – there are ways of giving them unity without starting again from scratch (see pages 42–45).

Another useful role that screens and boundaries can play in bigger gardens is as internal divisions to break up the space. You may have taken on a garden that is just one large space, perhaps mainly lawn with narrow borders round the edges, rather like the

ABOVE Witty barnyard cut-outs prevent this metal screen from being too overpowering. The purple-flowered vine offers a bold contrast with the orange paint.

PREVIOUS PAGE It's not what you use, it's the way that you use it. In this garden, broken concrete paving slabs have been used by garden designer Dan Pearson to create beautiful curving, sloping walls.

**ways with walls and fences / 39**

ABOVE **Alive, alive-o! This simple, but effective and pretty instant mosaic is made from cockle and mussel shells pressed into wet render.**

TOP **Bright Mediterranean-blue paint on this wall is an exciting backdrop for magenta bougainvillea.**

Mellow brick walls are an asset in any garden, but not all are brick, nor are they necessarily mellow. They might be of concrete or rendered. They may be dark and dirty, badly patched, of differently coloured bricks or even of different materials.

The easiest way to deal with ugly walls is with masonry paint. It covers a multitude of sins and at a stroke brings unity to the garden. But if your walls are in poor shape structurally, you should have them re-pointed or even rendered before you paint. If the walls are beyond hope and you can't afford to tackle them right away, panels of marine plywood painted with an exterior paint and pinned to the wall offer an instant, low-cost short-term solution.

When it comes to colour, consider the style of your garden. Soft pastels – blues, greens, lavenders – are best in a traditional garden while crisp neutrals – greys, stone, taupe – work well in a formal setting. Stronger tones such as ochre, terracotta and plum are best in contemporary gardens. White is a good choice for a southern climate: in the north, it is too harsh, especially in the grey winter months. Here, cream, soft yellow or beige are a warmer choice.

Colour also affects people's mood. 'Hot' colours such as red and orange are stimulating and energizing, and will make a space look smaller. 'Cool' colours – blues, mauves – are relaxing and will make a space look bigger. You need to think, too, about the colour as a backdrop for plants. Soft blues and greens work well with everything, while stronger tones look dramatic with a 'hot' planting scheme.

You can also use paint effects. Paint your walls with two tones of the same colour, for example, sponging or stippling one over the other. You could use stencils too, stencilling, say, an exotic creeper onto the wall or a more abstract design, such as bold shafts of sunlight sprayed on with metallic copper plastic aerosol paint. If you like the idea of a full-blown mural, you could hire an artist to create an eighteenth-century English landscape or a Tuscan countryside, perhaps 'propping' the mural with a pair of tall slender conifers, such as *Juniperus scopulorum* 'Skyrocket' in terracotta pots to link illusion and reality.

Another way of livening up dull boundaries instantly is with texture. Panels of trellis, for example, break up a plain surface and give a 3-D effect, creating patterns of light and shade. Parallel battens in differing lengths also create interesting patterns and shadows. Paint them the same colour as the wall for a subtle effect, or in a contrasting colour for a more dramatic one. You can also use stout galvanized wire to create geometric patterns on a plain surface – diamonds, zig-zags or fans. They will add interest immediately, and in the longer term, you could also grow small-leafed ivy along them, keeping it neatly clipped so that the shape remains sharp – a form of two-dimensional topiary.

You can now buy stylized cut-out decorative panels made from MDF that you screw onto the wall. They come in a range of designs – orange trees for example, or cypresses, or more complicated Moorish windows with ornate patterned grilles and a view beyond of minarets. Again, to link illusion and reality, a palm, or an orange tree in a pot in front of the wall, would be all you would need.

Gardens shouldn't take themselves too seriously, so have fun with them as well. One witty idea would be to use an old fireplace against the wall, and fill the grate with pots of black *Ophiopogon* for the coal, and bright orange and red flowering plants – crocosmia, zinnias, busy lizzies perhaps – for the glowing embers and flames. You could put objects on the mantelpiece, such as a pot of African violets, or some attractive seashells, and you could even hang a mirror – the type made specially for outside use – above it. Alternatively, use mirror to create a window, with glazing bars across it, and curtains of waterproof fabric or even fine stainless-steel chains.

ABOVE **A dull brick wall is enlivened not only by the soft blue-green masonry paint, but by the collection of galvanized metal objects hung on it and placed on the steps alongside.**

## new walls

**A**lthough walls are expensive, they are the most permanent form of boundary or screen. They provide security and privacy as well as, in small town gardens, a micro-climate for the plants. In larger, very exposed, gardens, walls can make problems rather than solve them, creating wind turbulence that damages plants in their lee. Here, a shelter belt of trees or shrubs outside the wall is the best solution.

Boundary walls are best left to builders who will take care of all the essential technical aspects; what you need to think about is the look.

In a small space, walls will dominate visually, so it is vital that they look good immediately. Ideally the materials should match those of the house. If your house is brick, then use bricks that match the colour as closely as possible, and if yours is an older property, consider using second-hand bricks. They are not cheaper, but they have a desirable weathered quality and will blend with the house very quickly.

Think about the style of the wall, the bond (the pattern in which the bricks are laid), the colour of the mortar and even the style of the pointing. You will be more conscious, for example, of an elaborate bond, of contrasting mortar and of deeply recessed pointing that shows up every individual brick than you will of something simpler, with mortar the same colour as the bricks and plain flush pointing.

Stone walls can be either formal or informal, urban or rural depending on whether you use 'dressed' stone – stone that has been cut into blocks – or rough 'undressed' stone. Again you need to consider the colour and style of the pointing.

In a modern setting, flat untextured rendered or concrete walls work very well, adding a strong sculptural element to the garden. It would be wasteful to render brick or stone since you don't see what is underneath, so instead use concrete or breeze blocks, which are much quicker and therefore less expensive to lay, and render those. Concrete, after years of being dismissed as strictly utilitarian, is making a comeback. It can be poured into a mould and coloured either with pigment mixed into the cement, or painted with masonry paint after it has set. It can be given different textures by the shuttering wood, and while boundary walls will need to be straight, there is no reason why internal concrete walls can't be curved or even wavy.

Other materials can be shaped successfully, too. British garden designer Bonita Bulaitis has used staggered triangular wall-like screens to create movement through a garden. Made from shaped, rendered breeze blocks, each has a round hole through which you can glimpse the planting on the other side.

It's also possible to make interesting sculptural walls using poured concrete.

Whatever the material you decide to use for your walls, scale is very important. A small garden with high walls all round can look like a prison exercise yard. A better option might be to make the walls lower – 1.5m (5ft) or even 1.2m (4ft) – with taller piers at regular intervals, and use trellis panels in between. Trellis always adds a strong architectural dimension to the garden and a design with small apertures gives almost as much privacy as a wall, but without the slightly claustrophobic feeling.

ABOVE **Old roof tiles make a delightful curved low wall to enclose this bench in its woodland setting.**

ABOVE CENTRE **The stark grid pattern of a wall made from textured aggregate blocks forms a stunning backdrop to a row of spiky architectural cacti.**

ABOVE LEFT **Poured concrete is ideal for curved walls, and the grey colour is the perfect foil for a silver-and-gold planting scheme.**

OPPOSITE **A modern combination of steel and opaque waterproof fabric makes a great screen and a background for a massed planting of delicate *Iris sibirica*.**

## new fences

ABOVE **A fence of hardwood planks, matching the decking, might be a little heavy in some settings, but works extremely well in this stark, minimalist garden.**

RIGHT **Woven willow withies make an organic screen that is attractive straight away. The bonus lies in the leafy growth that they make in summer.**

FAR RIGHT **Round poles of slightly differing heights stained a steely blue make an attractive textured screen that is quick to achieve.**

New fences are a less expensive and much faster option than new walls – a small garden could be fenced all round in only a couple of days. While they won't last as long as walls, well-constructed fences made from treated timber should last a good twenty years or so.

As with walls, the visual impact will be major, so the choice of fencing needs careful thought. Take your cue from the surroundings. In a country setting – a village rather than in open countryside – informal fencing such as woven willow or hazel hurdles would look good, as would palisades. These are stout poles either driven directly into the ground or fixed to arris rails that are in turn attached to fence posts cemented into the ground. For a more interesting textured look, try the 'hit and miss' style – with alternate poles either side of the arris rails. The bark can be left on for a chunky feel, or stripped and the poles then painted or stained for a slightly more formal look. The poles can be pointed at the tops – like a stockade – or rounded for a softer, less aggressive look. They can be cut in a wave formation, in broad castellations or left straight.

Bamboo makes a lighter boundary that looks good in rural and urban settings – where it works well with both contemporary and oriental styles. Use either stout canes, palisade style, thinner canes, split and wired together and braced at the back for support, or even a grid of canes, trellis fashion, tied together with non-perishable twine or even with thin strips of leather tied in ornamental knots.

In town gardens, close-boarded fences are the usual choice. They are available with planks running either horizontally or vertically. In the case of horizontal planks, the planks are often left uneven for a more informal look, while vertical planks can be either slightly overlapping – 'feathered' – or flush. If you have your fences custom-made (not that much more expensive than buying off-the-peg panels), you can have the tops shaped decoratively or you could have, say, diamond shapes cut out of each plank and then filled with pieces of copper or aluminium or even stained glass. British garden designer Dan Pearson once decorated the top of a fence with bright blue glass mineral water bottles pushed, neck first, into circles cut in the wood.

For fences in a contemporary garden, you could consider using square panels made from planks on the diagonal. These create a bold zig-zag pattern along the boundaries. Since they are so strong visually, they would work best in a fairly minimalist setting and would look most stylish if they were painted rather than stained. Obviously colour is a vital element when it comes to the impact new fences will have. See pages 42–43 to read about different colours and the effects they create.

When it comes to scale, the same rules apply to fences as to walls: in small spaces, fencing should not be too high. If you want height without too much sense of enclosure, panels of trellis fixed to the top of a solid fence offer a good solution. Trellis has the advantage of working well in every style of garden and it is available in many patterns. Rectangular trellis, for example, looks very crisp and modern.

You can also use stout trellis on its own. It makes a useful screen not only within the garden but also on the boundary, especially in very small spaces. It is not solid, of course, but even before plants start growing up it, it creates that all-important sense of privacy.

# east meets west

YOU WILL NEED FOR A 3M (10FT) SCREEN
• 21 x bamboo poles approx. 10cm (4in) in diameter
  and between 1.5m (5ft) and 90cm (3ft) long
• 35m (38yd) 'natural' polypropylene rope
• 21 x 2.5cm x 2.5cm (1 x 1in) wooden stakes 60cm (2ft) long

## chunky bamboo • flowing lines

One of the design problems in a small garden is that there is nowhere to go. You walk out into the garden and there it is, all laid out in front of you. That's that. One way of adding interest without making it feel much smaller is to divide it up with a not-quite-solid screen, part way across. That way you can glimpse what lies beyond, but there is an element of surprise.

To make our screen, we used extremely stout bamboo poles, spaced about the same distance apart as their diameter. We tied them together for both ornamentation and strength with polypropylene rope that resembles hemp but is much more durable.

The poles were cut to different lengths so the finished screen has a graceful curve, starting around 1.5m (5ft) high at the boundary fence and sweeping down across the garden. It also curves from back to front to accommodate the shape of the paved area at the end of the garden.

The simplest way to erect the screen was to hammer a series of pointed wooden stakes into the lawn. We then slotted a bamboo pole over each stake. To prepare the bamboo poles we had to first break through the thin internal membrane at each nodule so the bamboo would slide easily over the stake. Initially, the bamboo poles will wobble around the stakes, but once they are all tied together, they will be stable.

The knots, which are decorative as well as functional, can be as simple or ornate as you like. The Japanese have made an art form of tying bamboo poles together with rope or twine to make a screen. If you have a nautical bent or the Boy Scouts or Girl Guides featured in your past, tying the rope will be relatively straightforward. A tip is to wedge pieces of wood between the poles to keep them vertical and ensure that the tension is right as you work.

The rope will look particularly good if it follows the curve of the screen.

# at ground level

**F**rom the impatient gardener's point of view, all garden floors are ideal because they are virtually instant and they make a huge difference to the garden right away. For that reason, and because the floor will be even more prominent in winter, it is worth thinking about it as a decorative feature in its own right, not merely as the bits in between everything else.

As an impatient gardener you are likely to employ someone to do the work, but the decisions about the materials and the manner in which are they laid are yours and are very important because they will, to a large extent, dictate the style of your garden.

I say 'materials' because most gardens have more than one type of surface. While very small city spaces, whether backyards, roof terraces or courtyards, may have room for only one type of flooring, larger gardens will have more. In a garden that is largely lawn and borders, there will be at least one terrace or patio, and paths to enable you to move around the garden in all weathers.

Lawn, although technically 'soft' rather than 'hard', is none the less a garden floor and probably still the most widely used. In the form of turf, which can be laid instantly like carpet, rather than seed, which takes some weeks to grow, it is well-suited to the needs of the instant gardener. It works very well in traditional settings and there is no doubt that a sward of perfect emerald green sets plants off beautifully. It is the obvious choice for medium and large gardens, both rural and urban, where hard landscaping would be both inappropriate and financially ruinous. It is also the surface best suited to family gardens, where space for children to play is an important factor, provided the area of lawn is large enough. Small areas of lawn are just not practical in this situation because they take so much wear and tear that they never look good, and the inevitable bare patches will end up muddy in winter and baked hard in summer. In gardens like these, and in those where problems such as shade or large trees sucking all the moisture and nutrients out of the soil mean that an acceptable-looking lawn is simply not a realistic option, hard landscaping is almost certainly the answer.

Many people cling to lawn, no matter how dreadful it looks, because they fear that the only alternative is fence-to-fence concrete. But that simply is not the case. A mixture of hard landscaping and planting is a very attractive option. It is also very practical because you can use it when a lawn would still be soggy after rain, and, provided you choose plants that are easy to care for, much less demanding in terms of maintenance. As I have said, I am always amazed when people think that putting their whole garden down to lawn is an easy-care option. Beautiful lawns are a hobby rather than a garden floor, and a very demanding hobby at that.

Gravel, which is a fluid hard-landscaping material, can have an informal or Mediterranean feel about it or it can be formal, used with low clipped hedges to create a parterre effect. It is an ideal material for integrating the hard and soft elements within a garden because you can grow plants through and even in it. It's inexpensive, and is ideal for impatient gardeners because it is quick both to lay and to remove, so it can be a good temporary option to spread over soil, grass or, thinly, over an unattractive existing hard surface while you make long-term decisions about the garden floor. It also makes a very good permanent surface, laid over a well-compacted base, and can be used to great effect in combination with other hard materials such as York stone, bricks, setts, cobbles and so on.

Of course, all these materials can also be used on their own, informally or formally, depending on the finish and how they are laid. If cost is a factor and the real thing beyond your budget, then go for reproduction materials, which are looking better all the time.

OPPOSITE **This striking, 'fifties contemporary' style floor, seen mostly from above, is made from shaped concrete slabs and small white marble chippings. The curve of the paving echoes the curve of the spiral staircase.**

Limestone has long been used for paving, but as other forms of stone such as slate and granite are becoming increasingly popular as flooring materials inside the house, so they are beginning to be used in the garden too. In a small city yard, for example, dark limestone flooring with white-painted, rendered raised beds and just a few galvanized metal containers would look very modern and stylish.

Although poured concrete has a bad reputation, it is currently enjoying something of a revival among modern garden designers. It can be used to make any shape you like, as well as the more usual smooth, completely unbroken surfaces and it can be tinted with chemical dyes to produce a range of subtle or bold colours. It works best when it is unashamedly itself, and is not imprinted to mimic setts, cobbles or pavers.

Metal, a decidedly contemporary material, is also becoming more popular for city gardens, roof terraces and so forth. Chequered sheets of textured metal can be screwed to a subframe, just as wooden decking is, while a panel of industrial-strength steel grating could be very effective across water, forming a bridge. Metal is more suited perhaps to a temperate climate than to a very hot one where it could become uncomfortable, not to say painful, to walk on in the middle of the day in bare feet.

Wood, too, is becoming increasingly popular for garden flooring, especially in the form of decking. Although its critics say it is not a suitable material for use in a temperate climate, it works very well from a design point of view in a lot of situations, ranging from inner city backyards to more rural locations. As an attractive organic material, wood blends well with garden planting and is extremely versatile. If left to weather, it becomes a lovely soft silvery grey and looks old and rustic, whereas stained, it takes on a smart contemporary appearance.

Decking is in many ways the ideal flooring for an impatient gardener because problems with levels are resolved more easily than by using any other material. Decking can also be laid over existing surfaces. You don't have to dig out old cracked concrete first, nor do you have to consider those boring but essential details such as the level of the house's damp-proof course. Since air circulates freely through and under decking it doesn't matter if the decking finishes above the damp-proof course, whereas that would be of major

BELOW **Old floorboards recycled as decking have been given an added lift with stencilled oriental patterns, and have been weatherproofed with polyurethane varnish.**

importance with other materials. The same is true of rubber flooring designed for play areas but which makes an interesting colourful material for a garden too, either laid over an existing surface or from scratch over a firm base.

When it comes to choosing the materials, think about them in relation to the house. If the house or conservatory opens out onto the garden consider carrying the same material through from the interior. This will immediately give the house and garden a unity. Limestone, granite and slate would work well in this situation, and large terracotta tiles are also a possibility. They will give the garden an instant Mediterranean feel, though do make sure that you use frost-proof ones for outside.

If your house walls are brick, then consider using bricks of the same colour, if not for a whole patio perhaps, then as decoration – an edging, perhaps, or as a grid to frame panels of concrete slabs.

If you have an artistic bent and enjoy quick small-scale projects, you could adapt a Victorian design idea and make a couple of random mosaic panels instead. You could use anything from small coloured pebbles to fragments of broken china, very small brightly coloured ceramic tiles or even glass marbles or nuggets. Combining different materials often creates the most interesting surfaces, but make sure that you don't use too many materials because the result can look fussy and is distracting, especially in a very small space.

You also need to consider the scale of your chosen materials. One school of thought says that it is best to use the largest possible size of slabs in a small area because that results in fewer joints. The effect of this will be that the space will look less 'busy' and so it will feel larger. The other view is that where space is limited, very large units will look out of proportion, which will make the area look even smaller, while more compact units, especially if laid in a simple unfussy pattern, can make the space feel larger.

Certainly, more compact units are easier to lay, since you will need to do less cutting to make them fit. If you are planning to do the work yourself, then it is well worth basing the layout on the dimensions of your chosen materials wherever possible to avoid having to cut any at all. One point to bear in mind is that if the design you have chosen involves curves or circles, you will find small units much easier to work with than larger ones.

BELOW Fine, resin-bonded glass chippings, in yellow at the top of the mounds and grading through green to deep blue in the 'valley', are as much a work of art as a garden path.

# fantasy facelift

## YOU WILL NEED
- assorted marbles
- cement-based tile adhesive
- polystyrene cut to the same size as the space left by the lifted slab

## sparkling glass • light-as-air effect

Glass marbles or florists' nuggets are an attractive way of using glass in the garden. To replace our two paving slabs, we used a design of flame-coloured and yellow 'spaghetti' marbles (clear marbles with strings of colour in the centre), surrounded by small yellow and white crystal marbles.

Work out roughly how many marbles you will need from their diameter. Use a cement-based tile adhesive suitable for exterior use, and you'll have plenty of time to lay the marbles before the adhesive begins to set. Be sure to use white adhesive rather than grey.

The easiest patterns consist of marbles laid in rows, but if you want a more complex pattern, it's best to make a simple template. Cut a piece of polystyrene the same size as the space left by the slab. Draw your pattern on the polystyrene, cut along the edges of the design with a craft knife and remove the section you plan to fill first. Lay the template with the appropriate section removed over the space to be filled.

Mix up the adhesive, fill the space about two-thirds deep, then press the marbles into it. From time to time, lay a plank of wood over your work and press down gently until the ends of the plank are flat on the neighbouring slabs to ensure the mosaic is flush. When you have finished a section, leave the adhesive to set for ten minutes or so, then gently ease the template off. You may need to run a sharp knife around the edges to make sure it lifts off cleanly. Leave the adhesive to set completely overnight.

Next day mix up more adhesive and fill in the remaining spaces. Once it has set completely, scrub the marbles with an old toothbrush or nail brush to remove any stray adhesive.

One way impatient gardeners can give an old slabbed patio an instant face-lift is to replace a few of the slabs – especially any damaged ones – with a different material. For best results, make sure that the overall effect looks random.

You can use bricks to match the house, but in fact brick pavers are an easier option because they are thinner – the same thickness as standard paving slabs. This makes them very simple to lay in the space left by the slab. You just scrape out the old mortar and replace it with fresh without needing to excavate to a greater depth. Brick pavers can be laid in a herringbone pattern, forming a series of 'V's, or in a basket-weave design, with two pavers laid lengthways, then two widthways, and so on. Another option is to use cobbles laid end on or even side on, either packed closely together in rows or in a slightly more complicated pattern.

You may have access to old roofing tiles or slates. These, cut in half and laid side on, can make very attractive zig-zag or sunray patterns.

An even more artistic option would be to replace a few slabs with mosaic, using a variety of materials set in cement. In the nineteenth century, people were keen on using small coloured pebbles and seashells to make elaborate patterns. Given that they need to be placed

BELOW **Crazy paving that was originally grey, yellow and pink has been transformed with two shades of terracotta masonry paint, one sponged over the other.**

# quick fixes at ground level

ABOVE Break up a large expanse of plain paving by removing groups of pavers randomly and planting with spreading plants such as erigeron.

RIGHT Mixing crazy paving, brick and roofing tiles makes an attractive floor. Enliven an uninteresting surface by replacing a few slabs with materials like these.

in wet cement, it is best to work out your pattern on paper first and sort out the different coloured stones you need into piles so that once you start, you can work quickly. To make sure the mosaic is flush with the surrounding paving, press lightly down on it with a plank as you work.

For a modern look, you could replace a few slabs with metal or glass. Steel and brass washers in a variety of sizes can look very stylish, especially if laid at random and overlapping. So can large, beautifully patterned and coloured glass marbles, or even iridescent glass florists' nuggets, which are available in a range of vivid blues, greens, reds and golds. If you are using glass marbles or nuggets, make sure you set them in white cement rather than the usual grey. This will give a light, bright background and show off the colours at their dazzling best.

Planting is another option for adding interest to an existing patio. You can remove whole slabs, and plant in the space you have created, but on a small patio, large areas of planting can look a little out of proportion. A better option would be to remove part of a slab or a paver – use a cold chisel and bolster to take out a corner – and plant low-growing creeping alpines, which will soon spread over the edges of the planting hole and across the paving in a natural looking way. Evergreens such as carpeting thymes are the best value. These offer winter interest, have small pink, mauve, red or white flowers in early summer, and release their fragrance when they are stepped on.

Thrift (*Armeria maritima*) is another good choice, forming soft hummocks of long slender bright evergreen leaves with masses of bright pink clover-like flowers in summer. The New Zealand burr (*Acaena microphylla* 'Copper Carpet' syn. *A. m.* 'Kupferteppich'), which forms a carpet of tiny coppery leaves with small round spiky flowers of chestnut brown, looks very good with yellow bricks or setts.

You may inherit a patio or indeed a whole small garden made up of dirty stained concrete slabs, and while you do not intend to keep them long term, you cannot afford to replace them right away. What you can do is improve their appearance immeasurably with paint. It won't last indefinitely, but will make a big temporary improvement.

The first job is to clean the slabs, using a proprietary patio and path cleaner, which will remove layers of muck and grime and will make them look much better and brighter right away. Then you can paint them with step and tile paint, which comes in a fairly limited range of basic colours – stone, grey, brick red and so on. It is best to use a colour close to that

of the original slabs, so that as the paint does start to wear away eventually – not that you are likely to leave the slabs down long enough for that to happen – it won't look blotchy. Technically, step and tile paint is not recommended for outside use, but from personal experience I know that it will last long enough to do the job you want it to do.

Masonry paint, though fine for outside use, is not recommended for floors either, but, again from personal experience, I know that it works well. One garden where masonry paint was used to make a multi-coloured crazy paving effect on a large patio had over five hundred visitors walking on it during an open day, and the paint came through with no sign of wear and tear at all. Masonry paint comes in a much wider range of colours than step and tile paint. There are many shades of blue and green as well as beiges, browns and reds, so this type of paint offers more scope for artistic flair.

When it comes to choice of colour, one option would be to paint the slabs with a base colour such as terracotta or ochre and then stipple or sponge a darker or lighter shade of the same colour on top to create texture.

Another option would be to use a base colour, or even leave the surface as it is if the slabs are in an acceptable state, and then make patterns with a contrasting colour. You could use bold zig-zags as a border or indeed any geometric shapes around the edges, in one corner or right across the whole area. If you are doing it yourself, draw out the design on graph paper first and then transfer it onto the ground. If you use chalk, you can easily correct any mistakes. When you are happy with the design, mask the area not to be painted with newspaper and broad masking tape.

You could use stencils for smaller designs, either bought from a craft shop or home made. Obviously, simpler shapes such as circles, ovals and diamonds are easier to do and work best.

On a roof terrace where we created a jungle planting in containers, we used slightly curved triangles of three different sizes and warm earthy colours such as ochre and warm reddish brown to suggest – somewhat fancifully perhaps – patches of light on the jungle floor.

Equally, in a more contemporary setting, circles in bold bright 1960s colours such as acid green, orange and bright blue would look very stylish, either on their own or two together, the smaller overlapping the larger slightly. While you may not find these colours ready mixed, specialist shops that mix paints should be able to supply you with exactly the colours you want.

ABOVE **A chequerboard effect of concrete slabs and gravel, planted with irises can be more interesting than a plain concrete-slab floor.**

# new life for tired slabs

**YOU WILL NEED**
- stiff corrugated cardboard
- 2 x cans multi-surface garden paint in aerosol form
- 1 x terracotta bowl 20cm (8in) diameter
- copper acrylic all-surface paint in aerosol form
- 3 x *Echeveria elegans*

## sizzling stencil • funky furniture

This modern startling pattern of blue and orange circles cannot fail to liven up an area of old slabs. We used the design as a border, but it could be equally effective as a random pattern. All you need is some stiff corrugated cardboard and multi-surface garden paints in the colours of your choice. We used aerosols but you can also buy these paints in tins and paint them on with a stiff stencilling brush.

We started by cutting a template from the cardboard, the same size as a slab. The template consisted of three sections – the outer section, the large circle and the smaller circle cut out of the larger one. You will need to keep removing bits of the template, which is why it's best to use stiff cardboard.

To spray a blue circle, we placed the three-part template in position on a slab and removed the large circle, leaving the small circle and the outer section in place as we sprayed. Once the blue paint was dry, we replaced the large circle in the template, removed the small one and sprayed on the orange paint. We repeated these steps until the border was complete.

Our finishing touch was a simple terracotta bowl, sprayed with a copper acrylic all-surface paint, and planted with echeverias. These have fleshy blue leaves and tall slender sprays of bright orange flowers that complement the paint colours very well. Echeverias are not hardy, so bring them inside in winter where they make attractive houseplants.

As a finishing touch, this round orange plastic chair could not have been more perfect.

Natural stone is a superb paving material for the garden. Whether it is old and weathered or newly cut, it comes in a beautifully subtle range of colours from almost pure white to black, taking in everything from pinks, beiges, browns, purples and greys en route. It is also extremely hardwearing and, unlike so many other things, only gets better with age. Slate, granite, sandstone and carboniferous limestone (oölitic limestone is probably too soft for outside use) are all good choices, and if you live in an area that has its own local stone, it makes sense to use it, not least because it will help keep costs down.

Natural stone is very expensive, so while it may be an option for a very small garden, in a larger space, reproduction stone slabs may be a more realistic choice. Some years ago, they were a poor imitation of the real thing, but now they are greatly improved, especially the reconstituted stone types. These use ground natural stone in their manufacture, and are made in moulds based on natural stone slabs so that the surface texture is very realistic indeed. Before you commit yourself, do look at the colour of the slabs wet as well as dry, because it can change quite dramatically, and in temperate climates you will be seeing them wet a lot of the time.

It is also best to stick to one colour. Those chequerboard patios and paths in pink and yellow slabs, so popular in the 1970s and 1980s, unfortunately look like rhubarb and custard.

Both real and reproduction slabs come in different finishes, which create different effects. Dressed slabs have a smooth, in some cases almost polished, finish and perfectly straight edges, which means they work well in formal or modern gardens but would look out of keeping in an informal setting. Undressed slabs, which have a riven, textured surface and irregular edges, work well in an informal setting.

Undressed slabs can also look good in formal gardens depending on how they are laid. A simple clean geometric layout works best here, with the joints pointed with mortar. In an informal setting go for a looser design using slabs of different sizes with the edges unaligned and the joints left unpointed. You can fill the gaps with soil mixed with suitable seeds – erigeron, for instance, alyssum, or California poppies (*Eschscholzia*) – or wait for moss to colonize them for a relaxed weathered look.

Crazy paving is also an option for an informal garden. Buying off-cuts is certainly a less expensive means of using real stone, and even broken reproduction slabs can look good if they are well laid, with a generous amount of mortar in between and framed, for example, with lines of brick to create square or diamond-shaped panels.

For a modern garden, poured concrete can make an exciting, bold dynamic surface in whatever shape, texture or colour you like. Although any competent home handyperson or builder can lay concrete successfully, to exploit the design potential of the material fully, it is best to use a specialist company.

OPPOSITE **Surrounded by stark walls and simple stone paving, a pattern of differently coloured aggregates injects life into this boldly contemporary garden.**

BELOW **A combination of fine gravel and clean-cut slate slabs makes a very stylish path. The soft planting of alchemilla makes a striking contrast.**

**ground·level effects • stone and concrete**

ABOVE Small, square granite setts make an attractive informal surface in a confined space. Large pieces of granite placed in the border link the paving to the planting.

OPPOSITE Old terracotta 'pamments' or square pavers give instant maturity to a garden.

A strong current trend in modern garden design is to use materials within the garden that relate to the wider environment, and since the vast majority of us live in cities and towns – in other words, a built environment – what could be more suitable for flooring than brick? Since bricks are small units, they are extremely versatile, can be used to create many different patterns and shapes, and are able to fit into small and awkward spaces where larger units would present problems. Brick comes in a number of different colours from dark blue-black, through a variety of shades of red and brown to deep yellow ochre and even cream. You can use new or second-hand bricks. In an older property old bricks have the advantage of a weathered look, but they are not always readily available.

From a design point of view, it is best to match the bricks you use in the garden as closely as possible to those of the house, though the house bricks themselves may not be ideal. Some bricks are suitable for house building, but not for laying on the ground where they are liable to absorb water, expand as it freezes, contract as it thaws and then crumble as a result. Make sure you use frost-proof bricks. The hardest bricks of all are non-porous engineering bricks, which are often blue-black. These look very striking in a formal or modern garden, though they won't match the house walls.

Pavers, which have roughly the same visible dimensions as bricks when laid but are about half the thickness, are specially made for paving. Like bricks, they can be laid in a number of different patterns. Laid lengthways they add forward movement to a path or patio, leading the eye off into the distance. Laid widthways, they draw the eye out to the sides, emphasizing the width rather than the length and so making the whole space feel wider. Patterns such as basket-weave are static, in other words, they do not lead the eye in any particular direction, and so are more suitable for patios and other sitting areas.

Ideally, patterns should be interesting enough to be worth looking at in winter, when there is not much else to catch the eye, but not so busy as to be distracting. My own patio, for example, a large area of old yellow London stock bricks, consists of basket-weave panels framed by a grid of the same bricks laid widthways. It is sufficiently interesting to prevent what is a large area of brick from being monotonous, and yet subtle enough not to detain your eye for too long.

Setts, which are about 10cm (4in) square, are another useful, even smaller-scale material for formal and informal gardens. They are square blocks of granite, real or imitation, with a slightly rounded upper face and are good for intricate patterns, tight curves and circles. The fact that the tops are curved slightly makes for an interesting textured surface. They can be used for an entire area, as decoration to break up an area of slabs or as edging to contain gravel.

Tiles, both ceramic and real or reproduction terracotta, are a good choice for warmer climates, and provided they are frost-proof, they can create a distinctively Mediterranean or Latin mood in temperate climates. They are ideal for roof gardens, balconies and patios that lead directly on from a conservatory.

Gravel, or shingle as it is sometimes called, and large chunky stone chippings are extremely versatile materials, inexpensive and very quick to lay – useful in any garden setting. Although they are hard materials, they have a fluidity and softness that makes them ideal for linking organic elements – plants – and inorganic ones, such as buildings. They can be used for drives and parking areas, as long as they have firm foundations underneath, for paths or patios on a suitably well-compacted base, or may just be spread loose in borders to bring a uniform look to an area.

Gravel and chippings, which are chips off the stone block, are available in a wide range of colours, as you might expect, and the colours vary depending on the area where they are produced. Gravel is usually a mixture of colours. If you do not live in an area that produces its own gravel, choose a colour range that blends best with your house or with the other hard materials you plan to use in the garden. York stone for example would look best with cool grey tones, while warm golden tones would be better with yellow sandstone. Look at as many types as you can, both wet

and dry, since the mix of colours will be more prominent when they are wet.

Gravel comes in different sizes, from very fine to chunky. A medium grade is perhaps the most practical because it does not stick to your shoes and get walked into the house so easily. Also, cats find the stones a little too large and heavy to scratch in. On a slight slope, gravel, which is angular, is better than smooth round pea gravel, because the stones grip together and don't move as much.

For pedestrian traffic, gravel should be at most 2.5cm (1in) deep, otherwise it is uncomfortable to walk on and will ridge up. So either lay it on a firm foundation or use a weed-suppressing membrane underneath and stepping stones of another material as a path through it. Slabs, real or reproduction, square or round, would look good, as would squares of pavers laid in twos or fours in a basket-weave pattern or even wood – horizontal slices of railway sleepers, for example or stout, pressure-treated planks.

For modern gardens, crushed glass, which is laid in the same way as gravel, is a very stylish, though more expensive option. It comes in a range of bright colours such as violet and turquoise. It has been tumbled to remove all sharp edges, so it is perfectly safe. Smooth oval florists' beads are another option, but they are more expensive in large quantities.

Fine metal chippings or granules – aluminium and stainless steel – are another very smart possibility for a modern garden, as are crushed CDs.

All these materials are laid loose, albeit in some instances over a compacted foundation, but many of the finer grades of aggregate can also be bonded to a resinated base to give the appearance of gravel with none of gravel's disadvantages. Since bonded aggregate creates a very thin layer – about 6mm (¼ in) thick, it is a very useful instant treatment for existing areas of concrete, which, although patched or stained and unattractive, are basically sound. It can also transform virgin ground since, like concrete, it can be used to make exciting free-flowing shapes. It is possible to make bold patterns with differently coloured aggregates, working with one colour at a time and waiting until each has set.

ABOVE **Crushed green and white glass makes an attractive, restful foil for the planting – not dissimilar to lawn.**

OPPOSITE LEFT **This heavily patterned floor, made from different gravels, chippings and seashells, needs only very simple containers and planting.**

OPPOSITE RIGHT **Small white pebbles work very well with the smooth clean lines of a metal containe,r and are echoed in the large pebbles that serve as a mulch.**

OPPOSITE **A circle of logs makes a dramatic pattern as well as a contrasting organic frame around concentric circles of different hard materials.**

BELOW RIGHT **Decking squares can be laid on virtually any surface to make an instant patio. You can also take them with you when you move.**

BELOW **Railway sleepers cut to different lengths are used as stepping stones through gravel. By emphasizing the width, they make this garden appear to be wider.**

Timber decking, which has long been popular for garden floors in the USA, Canada and Australia, is becoming increasingly sought after now in northern Europe. What makes it such an ideal material for the impatient gardener is that it can be laid over existing surfaces, whether that is old stained concrete or the rather lurid paving slabs often laid by the developers around a brand-new house. And another advantage of using timber decking is that you do not need to worry about breaching the damp-proof course on the house walls as you do with other materials because the decking is laid with a gap between the decking and the wall so air can circulate freely.

Decking is a very versatile material in that it can be cut to fit even the most awkwardly shaped areas and it is also an excellent choice when you have huge differences in level to contend with. In the sort of garden that slopes steeply up from the house, for example, it would be very expensive and time-consuming to terrace the site in order to create a flat area at the top for sitting out. It is relatively straightforward, though, to construct a wooden deck at the top of the garden, supported on stout square posts and accessed by a flight of steps. With the addition of a simple balustrade for safety, the deck will provide not just a useful seating area but also a great view over the garden.

There are many different types of wood that are suitable for decking. Hardwoods such as teak and oak are very expensive but will last a lifetime. Pressure-treated softwoods are less expensive and can also last for many years. Some firms offer 25-year guarantees, others a lifetime guarantee.

You will need to make a choice between grooved and smooth decking and there is some debate as to which is preferable. There are those who think grooved decking is better on the grounds that it is less slippery when wet. But in fact the grooves fill with soil and debris unless regularly swept, quickly rendering them smooth, so the choice is really down to appearance at the end of the day.

You can also use recycled timber – old hard oak or soft pine floorboards, for example, or even dismantled pallets. Left untreated, the aged appearance of old floorboards is part of their charm, while recycled pallets can be stained so the wood is indistinguishable from new. Obviously, softwood that has not been pressure treated needs to be preserved in some way to prolong its life anyway, so either treat it with a clear preservative every few years, or with coloured wood stain, some types of which are specially formulated for decking.

Wood stains come in many good colours now, ranging from subtle silver greys to natural browns and more vibrant blues and yellows, but as with fences, think carefully about your choice because a large area of strongly coloured flooring will have enormous visual impact, especially in the winter.

The way the decking is laid will also make an impact. The joints between planks and the lines on grooved decking, are visually very strong, and can be used to your advantage to add interest and create changes of direction through the garden. Used lengthways, decking will take the eye forward and makes the space appear longer. Laid widthways or on the diagonal, it makes it seem wider, but diagonally laid decking is also more static, so this pattern is ideal for an eating or sitting area.

While railway sleepers are too thick and heavy to be used as decking, they can look wonderful as simple steps or raised beds. But be aware that old sleepers will have been treated with tar, which may affect plants. Try and obtain new, untreated, sleepers instead. These are available from some timber merchants.

# ground-level effects • wood

LEFT **A low mound of mind-your-own-business (**Soleirolia soleirolii**) makes an attractive substitute for grass. Keep it confined like this, though, as it can be invasive.**

Lawn is still the most widely used garden floor, and so although it is technically 'soft' it is best included here.

As an impatient gardener, you will of course opt for turf as it looks good the instant it is laid, but it will still be a few weeks before it has rooted into the soil, is growing strongly and can be walked on.

Choose the grade of turf that is most suitable for the way you plan to use the lawn. A very fine grade of turf looks best, although it needs a lot of upkeep. A tougher grade will take more punishment, though will not look quite so plush, while for a shady garden, choose a grade that will tolerate shady conditions.

Turf is best laid in autumn when there is still some warmth in the soil, but there is likely to be plenty of rain, or in early spring, as the soil begins to warm up and there is also likely to be plenty of rain. You can lay it in summer, but then you will need to make sure it is watered regularly, or the joins may open up and ugly gaps appear.

In very small gardens, as I have already pointed out, lawn is not a practical surface because it is not very hard wearing (see page 53). But if you still want lawn because you like the way it looks or the way it feels beneath your feet, then use it in combination with hard materials that will take most of the wear and tear. You could place stepping stones through it, for example, made either of slabs or brick, or you could surround it with broad direct paths so that you are not tempted to take a short cut across the lawn.

In a formal setting, two or four squares of lawn surrounded by paving would both look very striking and be practical. Set stepping stones or paving just below the level of the grass so that the mower can skim over the whole lot, removing the need for time-consuming edge-trimming. In larger gardens, where you can have a decent sized lawn, installing a mowing strip of bricks, pavers or even slabs around the edge works in exactly the same way. These also form a useful barrier between lawn and plants, which can be inclined to flop over it and kill off the grass underneath. If you like the look of irregular slabs of York stone adjoining a lawn, be prepared to keep the edges trimmed with scissors!

Chamomile and thyme are sometimes suggested as alternatives to grass, but in large spaces they are a considerable amount of work in the early stages in terms of weeding and so forth. In small areas, though, surrounded by hard materials, they are easier to maintain. Neither plant minds being trodden on occasionally, and indeed, when crushed, they release their fragrance, but they would not make a suitable surface for family picnics or energetic games. Corsican mint is another possibility, especially in shade. It has minute pale mauve flowers and very small round green leaves that smell powerfully of peppermint when touched or walked on.

OPPOSITE **This textured lawn is very striking and is an idea that is quick and easy for an impatient gardener to copy.**

# features for added impact

**F**eatures are what give gardens character, turning a reasonably attractive garden into one that is special. They are particularly important to the impatient gardener because they make an immediate difference and, by drawing attention to one part of the garden, stop you focussing on the areas you haven't yet got around to dealing with.

But there is a delicate balance between instant gratification and the longer term. You don't want to invest time and money in a feature only to find later that it is in the wrong place or compromises your garden design. So even though you haven't got time to tackle the whole garden at once, do think about how it might all work eventually.

You will certainly need a patio close to the house, and the entrance to the garden from the house is also fixed, so you would be safe creating a feature there. Equally, you will only have one corner of the garden that catches the last rays of the sun, so you are likely to want a seating area there. Alternatively, when you start, stick to features that are not fixed, such as furniture, a sculpture or some plants in containers.

Features used as focal points will direct the eye to where you want it to go but make sure only one focal point is in view at a time, otherwise the impact will be lost. That is not

to say you can't have more than one focal point. By careful placement, you can even use a series of focal points to lead your visitors right round the garden. In very small gardens, especially those that are broader than they are long, site features with care and avoid anything too eye-catching on the far boundary because it will make the space appear even smaller than it is. Instead, create interest in the foreground.

Garden buildings – whether ornate summerhouses or garden sheds – are one type of permanent garden feature. Summerhouses may sound rather grand, but it is possible to find them at a size and price suitable for most gardens, and they not only add weight to the overall design of the garden, but also provide a sheltered place to sit, even on days that are bright but cold. If you want your summerhouse to blend in, paint it the same colour or perhaps a shade darker or lighter than the surrounding greenery or boundaries. If you want to make it a focal point, use a contrasting shade. Sheds are functional, but that does not mean they have to be ugly. Rather than hide them behind a screen, paint them an attractive colour to make a statement – beach-hut blue-and-white stripes in a gravel garden, for example, or rich Harrods green with gold fittings.

Pergolas and arbours are other garden features that add height and structure. They are also important to the way you use and enjoy your garden, giving you the sense of being inside while you are outside. And they help create a feeling of privacy, which, in overcrowded cities with neighbours so close by, is invaluable. Pergolas are particularly important when you are overlooked. While you may be seen through the gaps between the overhead beams, even when these are covered with plants, you feel enclosed and protected none the less. The same is true of arbours over seats. While you can have an arbour that is completely enclosed with solid timber or trellis, even a light structure of poles, ropes or netting creates a haven and makes you feel safe from prying eyes.

Pergolas can also suggest movement around the garden, dividing it up and yet linking different areas. And enclosing part of your garden with a pergola makes the spaces at either end feel more open and therefore larger. A simple arch or two can have a similar effect. Arches create a sense of somewhere to go – important in a small space where there are usually no surprises and the tendency is to see the whole garden at once the moment you step out through the door.

Water features bring at least two important dimensions to the garden: movement and sound. Even still water features add movement in the form of reflections of the clouds, plants moving in the wind or ripples across the surface. Or a handsome shallow bowl filled with water, especially if the interior is dark, creates wonderful reflections, and by suggesting infinite depths takes your mind beyond the garden. The sound of water is wonderfully relaxing, especially in busy towns and cities. Even an all-in-one, re-circulating ceramic wall mask and basin, which can be fitted on a balcony or roof garden in ten minutes, will create gentle splashing sounds to help divert your attention from traffic noise below. Water also attracts a whole range of wildlife – birds, frogs, newts, dragonflies and so on – often within days, if not hours after the water feature is installed.

If features such as pergolas and arbours are the furniture of the garden, then objects are the finishing touches that give it personality. These can be natural – boulders or pieces of driftwood, for instance – or man made – figurative or abstract pieces of sculpture, old implements, industrial or high-tech machine parts. Objects can bring wit and humour into the garden but, of course, humour is a very personal thing. That said, however, old lavatory pans are never funny!

Lighting cannot only be a feature in itself, but at night can enable you to enjoy all the other features in your garden, whether you are sitting outside or simply looking at the garden from indoors. It can be as simple or as complicated as you like – real flames from candles or lanterns, or electric lights, either low-voltage systems you can install yourself or the more sophisticated lighting that needs to be installed by a professional. Either way, you will be astonished by the pleasure lighting will provide.

OPPOSITE **Different forms of lighting transform this garden at night – the illuminated sculpture on the wall, the diffused lighting behind the panel of glass bricks, and the fairy lights on a mesh covering the roof and side of the pergola.**

pergolas

ABOVE **This very chunky pergola made from telegraph poles and thick timber is assertive enough to compete with the landscape beyond.**

Originally developed as frameworks to support vines in hot climates and create essential shade for the house, pergolas have become an important feature in the design of temperate gardens as well, where their main function is structural and decorative. They make ideal features for impatient gardeners, since they add instant height and structure to a garden.

They can be attached to buildings, making a useful visual link between house and garden, erected over paths to create movement through the space, or can be free standing as a feature over a seating area, perhaps, or a point where two paths cross. In a very small garden, they are best attached to the house or to a side wall rather than free standing, since they would take up too much space.

As for materials, the choice should be dictated by the style of your garden and, if the pergola is attached to the house, by the style of the house, too. Although in larger gardens stone or brick piers with wooden overheads were popular in nineteenth- and early twentieth-century gardens, wood is the most common choice these days since it is relatively inexpensive and quick to put up. In an informal garden, away from the house, natural-looking rustic poles have a cottage garden feel, but close to the house, and certainly in more formal gardens, square posts are better. You can make them look even smarter by chamfering the corners and painting or staining them either a dark colour – navy or black – or a pale blue-green or grey.

The style of the overheads plays an important part in the overall effect. Square timber left plain would give

a solid chunky feel, while thinner timbers, half-jointed to form a grid, are more elegant, especially if the ends of the timbers are shaped.

In modern gardens, you can use a wide range of industrial materials to stunning effect. Scaffolding poles, for example, can look very dramatic, as can welded square-section metal, used in the construction industry, or reinforced steel joists painted with tough external-grade enamel.

You could also use metal combined with wood. Lengths of copper piping, for example, make striking overheads for a wooden pergola, giving a lighter more airy feel than wooden overheads. Stainless-steel chain or cable would have a modern industrial-techno feel. For something more organic in appearance, use stout ropes, either natural or coloured. I say 'natural' but in

fact it is best to use polypropylene rope, which looks like hemp, rather than the real thing, because it will not rot, shrink or stretch. Alternatively, use lengths of stout bamboo as overheads, either left their natural colour or stained in a rich mix of colours – reds, ochres and oranges, for example. Again these have a lightness that timber lacks, and their contours make an interesting contrast with the strict geometry of the timber posts.

As for size, your pergola must be tall and wide enough for people to walk under and through it even when it is clothed with plants. If it is attached to the house, it will feel more integrated and less of an afterthought if its proportions bear some relation to those of the house. The width between the uprights, for example, could be the same as the width of a window or of the gap between windows.

ABOVE **A series of informal arches made from hazel poles creates a fragrant sweet pea tunnel. Fewer arches would make a very attractive arbour.**

## arbours

Traditionally, an arbour was a leafy bower, made from densely planted trees or shrubs trained together overhead to create a private, shady place to sit. Now, the term is more widely used to describe any enclosed seating area, where plants, although still important, no longer form the structure.

Gazebos were primarily ornamental, adding structure to the garden or framing a statue. They are usually round or octagonal in shape, so they need to be in an open prominent position, rather than tucked away in a corner or against a wall as an arbour would be. Gazebos are better suited to groups of people rather than individuals or couples since they are larger than arbours and they are normally sited in a more exposed position.

It is quite simple to buy both gazebos and arbours off the peg, either ready to install or in easy-to-assemble kit form.

Some arbours are solid timber, rather like sentry boxes, either rectangular or arched, plain or fancy, double or single, and often with a built-in seat. Stained or painted, they are very striking visually and have instant impact – ideal for the impatient gardener. Others are made from trellis panels, the degree of enclosure depending on the spaces between the battens, at least until climbing plants are well established. Those made from simple squared trellis have a less formal look than those made of thicker diamond or patterned trellis, where the slats are cut to create stars or 'square in a circle' shapes.

Metal frames are popular, too, especially the lightweight maintenance-free black nylon-coated aluminium types. You could adapt an arch to make an arbour against a wall, or use a purpose-made arbour. The latter is ideal for tucking into a mature border among existing trees and shrubs, which can be trained over the structure. A weeping tree such as the silver-leafed pear or the weeping birch is ideal. Since the framework is black it soon disappears into the background, leaving you with a green cave.

Woven willow or hazel also makes attractive arbours. Hazel, being thicker, looks best in informal gardens, while willow, being thinner and smoother, makes very clean shapes that can work well in a formal setting. You can leave them unpainted or give them a wash of colour – pale grey or even white looks very stylish, like woven cane furniture. If you want an oriental-style garden, a simple black framework, infilled with panels of split-bamboo or split-reed screening, could look very smart.

In a modern garden, unashamedly modern materials such as polycarbonate panels, especially used in conjunction with steel uprights, would make a striking arbour – sheltered from the wind, private and yet filled with light because the panels are translucent rather than transparent.

If all you are looking for is an impression of enclosure, you can make an arbour very simply using upright posts or poles linked with lightweight overheads – rather like a mini-pergola. To support the climbing plants, weave lengths of rope over the framework or even use ready-made cargo netting made of coarse rope. Nylon mesh is another option, but is not as attractive.

ABOVE  **A** simple metal framework, almost hidden by climbing plants, makes a delightful arbour above a rustic bench.

LEFT  Informal elements are given a degree of formality in this arbour. Clumps of soft catmint are planted symmetrically either side, while a rambling golden hop, clipped to be contained inside the arbour, contrasts with the scrambling white roses above.

# romantic arbour with a contemporary twist

## YOU WILL NEED

- 4 x uprights 100 x 100mm (4 x 4in) treated timber to required height, plus extra for fixing in the ground
- 4 x cross pieces 100 x 100mm (4 x 4in) treated timber to required width and depth
- 5 x lengths copper piping to required width plus overhang
- 4 x ball finials
- copper spray paint
- wood paint or stain for outdoor use
- 2 x large *Trachelospermum jasminoides*
- 1 x *Spiraea nipponica* 'Snowmound'
- 1 x *Polystichum tsussimense*
- 6 x *Lilium regale*
- 12 x *Nicotiana alata*
- 12 x white *Impatiens*
- 3 x small *Mentha requiennii*
- cocoa shells for mulching
- 1 x softwood bench treated with preservative then painted

## blue paint • soft planting

Creating an arbour in a small almost bare garden not only gives you somewhere pleasant to sit, it also makes a very attractive focal point to look at from the house. This small garden had only one feature – a very small shed tucked into the far corner. This seemed the ideal spot for an arbour.

Our design was very simple – uprights and crossbeams of 10 x 10cm (4 x 4in) timber with a 'roof' made from copper tubing finished at the corners with wooden finials sprayed with copper paint. Although, practically speaking, the roof does not provide shelter from the rain, psychologically it creates a sense of enclosure and privacy – especially important since the garden is overlooked from the rear. We stained the timber with a soft grey-blue opaque woodstain, which worked especially well with the copper. The same wood treatment was applied to the inexpensive self-assembly two-seater bench which was placed inside the arbour.

The planting scheme was green and white, which always looks cool and elegant. To scramble up the posts of the arbour, and eventually over the roof, we planted two large star jasmines (*Trachelospermum jasminoides*) – a superb evergreen climber with attractive glossy leaves and very fragrant white jasmine-like flowers in summer. To one side, we planted a *Spiraea nipponica* 'Snowmound' – a low-growing shrub with arching branches that are covered in clusters of small white flowers in late spring and early summer. On the shadier side of the arbour we planted an attractive fern (*Polystichum tsussimense*). This has very finely divided fronds, which it retains during mild winters.

Fragrance is an important element for an arbour, so all around the bench we planted groups of the beautiful, sweetly scented regal lily (*Lilium regale*). For immediate impact in the first season, we planted tall white tobacco plants (*Nicotiana alata*), which are deliciously fragrant in the evening, and for ground cover, we used white busy lizzies. Under the seat, where it is cool and shady, we planted Corsican mint (*Mentha requienii*). This will form a creeping carpet of tiny fresh green leaves that release a powerful mint smell when touched – cooling on a hot day to rub your feet on as you sit on the bench.

**W**hen it comes to choosing garden furniture, you need to weigh up both practical and aesthetic considerations. Seats must be comfortable and tables sturdy. They must be easily moved and stored if they are not weatherproof, and in very small gardens, particularly, they have to look good because they will be a very prominent part of the scene.

The materials are the same for all styles of garden – wood, metal, stone and plastic. It is the way they are used that makes the difference.

Wooden benches, chairs and tables in an informal cottage-style garden should be relatively plain. You can buy them in hard or softwood. Hardwood can stay outside in winter and will last for many years. If you oil it regularly it will keep its glossy brown colour, otherwise, it will weather to a silvery grey. Pressure-treated softwood is less expensive and will not last quite as long, although regular treatment with coloured woodstain or opaque paint will prolong its life.

Choose a colour that either blends or contrasts with the structures in your garden, though avoid too stark a contrast in very small gardens. Even a random collection of old kitchen chairs looks good painted all the same colour or in two or more complementary shades. If you like very bright colours, perhaps the answer is to paint the furniture in somewhat muted shades and add brightly coloured cushions.

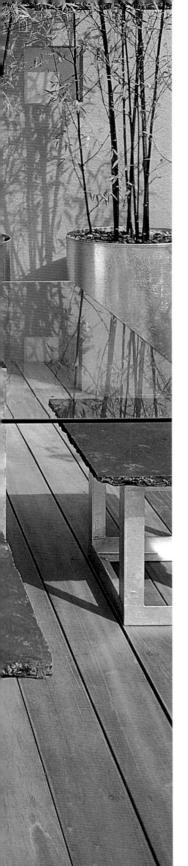

In a formal setting, Lutyens or Chinese Chippendale benches look good with tables and chairs in strong geometric shapes, while wooden furniture for modern gardens should have simple clean lines – angular or curved. Curved wood furniture is expensive as it is achieved by lamination and steaming.

Metal alone or a mixture of wood and metal can be informal, formal or contemporary according to the design. Reproduction cast-aluminium tables and chairs work well in informal settings and unlike the cast-iron originals are lightweight and don't need much maintenance. They come in white or mid-green, but you can paint them any colour you like, either with a plastic spray paint or with external enamel paint. They can also work in formal gardens, though simpler shapes and darker, more muted colours work best here.

In contemporary gardens, stylish metal tables and chairs in bright aluminium are fun, as are café chairs with metal frames and seats of plastic slats in 'contemporary' colours such as lime green or orange. If storage space is a problem, fold them up and hang them on the garden walls as art. Seats moulded from polypropylene in bold free-form shapes and bright colours are surprisingly comfortable and very sculptural when not in use.

As for ordinary plastic garden furniture, it is certainly the cheapest to buy and if that's all your budget runs to right now, treat it with an acrylic undercoat and spray it an interesting colour with plastic spray paint.

OPPOSITE  These stools and the pedestal table, which is cemented into the patio, are made from pressure-treated larch and have a simple chunky charm.

LEFT  Galvanized metal with glass and slate makes very striking contemporary furniture for a garden.

BELOW  Simple, widely available 'café' chairs and table work in almost all styles of garden. They have the advantage of folding for easy storage.

**N**othing brings a garden to life like water. A pool can replace lawn as the garden's calm centre, setting off the planting around it. Its reflective surface brings light into the space, which is especially useful in shady gardens. Be bold with pools and make them as large as possible. The impact is so much greater and, besides, large pools are easier to maintain.

Water features can be instant so are ideal for the impatient gardener. For an informal garden, you could make a barrel pond on the patio in no time at all. Put a layer of gravel or pebbles in the bottom of a barrel, add a couple of aquatic plants in their plastic baskets and a bunch of oxygenating weed, and fill with water. With a little more effort – you will need to dig a hole to hold the reservoir and low-voltage pump – you could create a bubble fountain. Once it is in place, cover the lid of the reservoir with pebbles, stone chippings, crushed glass or florists' nuggets. Alternatively, you can buy a ready-made water feature consisting of an old-fashioned hand pump pouring water into a barrel.

In a formal garden, a re-circulating wall fountain is ideal. All you need to do once it is fixed to the wall, is add water and plug it in.

An even simpler idea is to fill a large shallow bowl with water, add a few iridescent glass nuggets for sparkle and stand it in a sunny position on the patio. A bird bath also makes an attractive focal point, or with a little more work – again digging a hole for the pump and reservoir – and using a bowl with a hole in the bottom, you could create a simple fountain with a jet just high enough to make ripples on the surface.

Metal and water make an ideal combination in a modern garden, as do water and glass. A shallow container in steel or thick glass – or even concrete, a material that is suddenly back in fashion – would look wonderful. With a little more effort, so would a large metal or glass sphere set over a reservoir. Surface tension will make the water, which is pumped up through the hollow centre, cling to the sides all the way down, making the surface alive with the subtle movement of the water catching the light.

LEFT **Water and mirrors**
**are a magical combination**
**– the former adding**
**movement to the latter,**
**the latter adding light to**
**the former.**

# bowled
# over

## YOU WILL NEED
- 1 x large shallow container
- decorative glass marbles in blue, ice blue and white

## blue reflections

For a truly instant water feature, all you need is a very large shallow dish or bowl. Ours was made from galvanized metal about 60cm (2ft) across and 15cm (6in) deep. On the bottom, we placed glass marbles in rich blue, ice blue and white, which make the water appear cool and inviting – a little like the effect of turquoise tiles in a swimming pool.

Other materials would work as well – glossy black and white pebbles, for example, bright plastic granules or white sand with shop-bought sea shells (don't collect them yourself). Or you could make a textured and coloured design on the bottom of the bowl. Paint on waterproof adhesive in the design you want, then sprinkle on coloured sand or glitter. When it has dried, simply tip out the surplus and fill the bowl with water.

While it is not possible to grow aquatic plants in this bowl – it is too shallow and the metal would heat up in the sun too much – you can float cut flowers on the surface. Open daisy-like flowers are ideal – pot marigolds, osteospermums or gerberas for example. Change the water frequently to keep it clean and to stop algae growing in it.

If you are determined to grow plants in your water feature, then choose a container a minimum of 30cm (1ft) deep, such as a glazed pot without a drainage hole, or a watertight wooden barrel. Drop in a plastic mesh aquatic basket filled with either garden soil or aquatic compost (but not with ordinary potting compost, which is too rich in nutrients) and a dwarf water lily such as *Nymphaea* 'Pygmaea Helvola'.

fiddly ones. If you plan to keep fish, the pool needs to be at least 60cm (2ft) deep so that they can escape from predatory birds and from ice if the water freezes in winter. A shelf around the side of the pool about 30cm (1ft) down enables you to grow attractive marginal plants in baskets as well as deep-water plants and oxygenators to keep the water healthy. Dense planting helps to blur the edges of the pool and make it blend in with its surroundings in a naturalistic way.

If your garden is paved, of course, then it is impossible to make a natural-looking pool. Instead, go for a formal shape and plant it densely to give it that air of informality.

Formal pools, whether sunk into the ground or raised above ground level, should be strong geometric shapes – square or rectangular, ideally, or circular. The geometry is important here so it is best to leave them unplanted. Although water lilies, with their flat plate-like leaves, do not blur the lines, they do interfere to some extent with the reflective quality of the water. For the best reflections, either use black pond liner, or better still, since dealing with excess liner at the corners of a pool is very difficult, have the inside rendered and painted with black pond paint.

If you feel a formal pool would take up too much space, consider creating narrow rills or channels, no more than 25cm (10in) wide or deep, to dissect the garden – an idea that originated thousands of years ago in Persian 'paradise gardens'. Because the Persians believed the universe was divided into four quarters, the earliest paradise gardens were divided into four by rills. These could run parallel or intersect; each one would need its own reservoir and pump to keep the water flowing.

Another idea would be to have a much broader rill filled with rows of widely spaced setts with water flowing between them. Although it would look as though you were walking on water in fact your feet would remain dry.

In a modern garden, a similar idea with small oblong or cross-shaped pools set into a smooth surface such as concrete or resinated aggregate and lined with mirror-like aluminium looks stunning. Again metal and water are an ideal combination. A stainless steel chute, or a reinforced steel joist (RSJ) set in a smooth rendered wall, pouring a sheet of water into a slender rectangular pool looks very striking. You could also use RSJs painted bright colours with exterior enamel paint and set into paving to create instant shallow rills. A reservoir and pump concealed at one end would keep the water flowing.

LEFT **A simple, square galvanized tank filled with large stones and glass balls doesn't need any aquatic plants to make it look good.**

OPPOSITE LEFT **This modern water feature combines textured glass, metal, pebbles and wood. Simple geometric topiary in pots is all the planting you need.**

OPPOSITE RIGHT **This water feature on two levels has water flowing from the upper pool to the lower one, creating both sound and movement. It consists of two tanks, faced with chunky timber.**

Although they take a little longer to make than the instant water features on the previous pages, pools are still comparatively fast and have a huge impact right away.

Again, the style of garden will dictate the kind of pool that will work best. In an informal garden go for a natural-looking pool. While you can buy stiff pre-formed fibreglass liners, these always look unnatural, so it is best to use a flexible pond liner and make your own shape – with free-flowing curves rather than lots of

# lighting

ABOVE LEFT **Underwater lights throw stepping stones across a pond into sharp relief at night.**

ABOVE RIGHT **Boxy, modern plastic lights, reminiscent of Japanese paper lanterns, are particularly striking positioned as a group.**

OPPOSITE **Pools of light from uplighters set in the decking and beneath an ornamental grille add drama and mystery to this garden at night.**

**M**any people who go out to work get little opportunity to enjoy their gardens because for much of the year it is dark by the time they get home. The use of lighting can change all that, reclaiming the garden from the night and turning it into a magical theatrical place. In fact, it may look even better at night because you can highlight the very best bits and hide the less good ones under a forgiving cloak of darkness – especially important for the impatient gardener who may only have improved one area of the garden so far. Since lighting can be so important, it is well worth thinking about it from the start rather than adding it as an afterthought once the garden is finished.

What you are not aiming to do is flood the whole garden with light. (If you do want to install sensor-triggered security lighting, put that on a separate circuit.) You want to manipulate the space with light, and give features, plants, textures and colours a different dimension.

As a general rule, lighting works best in the garden if there are lots of small sources of light rather than just a few large ones, and if the fittings are hidden, either in among foliage or set flush into paving.

Spotlights are ideal for emphasizing the star features of the garden – a piece of sculpture, perhaps, a handsome bench or a particular tree or shrub. Statues or particularly ornate urns or pots are best lit from the front so that the detail is revealed. If they are lit from behind, you tend to get a silhouette. Side lighting is best for an object whose three-dimensional shape is its outstanding feature, such as a simple pot or an abstract sculpture. Trees, especially those with gnarled trunks and branches or attractive bark, look fantastic lit from below, their tracery of branches

standing out against the darkness. They look even more dramatic in winter when they have no leaves.

Walls look wonderful lit from below with wall washers, either highlighting the texture of brick or stone or creating texture on a plain rendered wall. Around an eating area, for example, uplighters on the walls would create a soft background glow, and all the additional light you would need for practicality could come from candles on the table.

You also need to consider the impact that shadow has. An architectural plant lit from below will cast fantastic magnified shadows on a nearby wall. In my own garden, the shadows cast by the jagged blue leaves of *Melianthus major* look like palm trees on a terracotta wall and turn south-west London at night into southern California.

You can use light to emphasize the style of your garden. In a formal garden, for example, narrow beams of light at regular intervals shining up a wall would add to the formality, while softer more diffuse lights set at different angles and washing over the wall would give a much more informal feel. In modern gardens, the latest technology in fibre optics, as well as neon, takes lighting into the realm of art.

You can also use uplighters to mark a path in a more subtle way than by using lanterns, while sidelights are ideal for illuminating steps or other changes of level.

Downlighters create discreet pools of light, which is another useful subtle way of marking features such as steps. These can be low enough for the fittings to be hidden in part by planting, or they can be very effective used as 'moon lights' high up in trees, shining down through the branches.

RIGHT **Candles in glass jars are a very simple but effective way of marking a route through this garden at night.**

FAR RIGHT **Tiny fairy lights, suitable for outdoor use, add sparkle to this clipped French lavender at night. They are small enough not to be intrusive in the daytime.**

Light and water – moving water especially – is a magical combination. Even a simple bubble fountain or wall mask becomes a star attraction at night as the light turns each dancing droplet to gold or silver. Uplighters work well underwater in a formal pool, especially if they are placed directly under a fountain or jet. Do avoid the multi-coloured pond lights on sale in most garden centres because they look more appropriate for a disco than a garden, and turn plants the most peculiar shades. Stick to white for a much more subtle effect.

Downlighters should also be avoided with any pond because they reveal all the mechanics – cables, pumps, pond liners – and of course any debris in the water. They also create an uncomfortable glare. Side lighting for both formal and informal pools is a good option because it creates strong shadows from the planting and turns a still surface into a mirror, giving you great reflections.

While you can install low-voltage DIY lighting yourself, you will need a qualified electrician for anything else, especially near water. Since lighting your garden is not just about the practicalities but about aesthetics too, it is worth employing a professional to design the layout. A good designer will come with a set of lights to demonstrate how the garden could look at night.

For instant lighting effects – for example for a special occasion, or while you are waiting for a permanent layout to be done – use low-voltage Christmas lights specially designed for outside use. Drape them over statues or obelisks, or over the branches of trees or shrubs. There is now a wide range of styles available – strings of little round pea

LEFT  Tea lights inside fire-resistant paper lanterns give off an appealing warm glow. They are especially striking in an informal group.

FAR LEFT  Candles pushed into sand or into the soil in flowerpots are an instant, inexpensive form of garden lighting.

lights, for example, light-emitting diodes (LEDs) in flexible plastic tubing, or fibre-optic cables. While white would be sophisticated and something you could leave in place all year, single colours – green blue, red or yellow – or perhaps two colours – blue and yellow, for example – would be fun for a party. Either have them on permanently or set them to twinkle or 'chase' each other. This is particularly effective when you use white light along the branches of a bare tree. Most of these lighting sets come with a programmer and a number of programming options.

For really quick temporary lighting, try candles, ranging from large flares on stout canes – ideal to illuminate a path – to versatile tea lights. You can use these in glass and metal lanterns to hang in trees or in glass storm lanterns on the table. Or you can use them *en masse* inside jam jars to light a path or along the top of a wall or in a large group on the patio floor – the more you have the more magical the effect. For a colourful approach, paint the outside of the jam jars with translucent glass paint (available from craft shops). Choose red or gold for warmth, or blue for a cooler effect. Alternatively, use the tea lights in large stiff brown paper sacks part-filled with sand for stability. They will cast a lovely warm golden glow. Either use wide sacks to reduce the risk of the paper catching fire or buy special sacks treated with a fire-retardant. Some of these have cut-out patterns of stars or half moons through which the candlelight shines. They look very festive.

For a pool or pond, try special floating candles. The flames are reflected in the water and the slightest movement makes both real and reflected flames dance and sparkle.

**objects**

**O**bjects, almost more than anything else, can stamp your personality on the garden, distil its essence and create a mood. For the impatient gardener, they are ideal because all that is required in most instances is a bit of careful thought about where to place them to best advantage. Objects have a permanence in the garden that plants do not have, but that is not to say they are unchanging. Pieces of sculpture, figurative or otherwise, change according to the light at different times of day and different times of year. They will be a different colour wet or dry and, if they are placed among plants, will take on more or less prominence according to the seasons.

The most useful rule of thumb when choosing large objects is that they should be strong, simple and few in number. As with any focal point, too many only confuse the eye and diminish the impact.

The type of sculpture you choose depends not only on the style of your garden but on your bank balance. Antique stone classical figures are very expensive – too expensive to risk leaving outside – but there are very good quality reproductions available, which look fine in a formal setting. There are also less expensive slightly rougher concrete versions, which would none the less work well in a less formal setting, especially after a bit of 'distressing' and being placed among plants. If you are determined to have a piece of antique stone in your garden, but a statue is beyond your pocket, investigate architectural salvage yards for ornate finials, broken pediments, chunks of column or even pieces of statue – a severed head or even a pair of feet can look very good, especially if dignified with a plinth.

Animal sculptures – bronze geese, chicken-wire sheep, even rusting metal hippos – can also work well, but they must be aesthetically pleasing in their own right and/or great fun. You may think rabbits pushing wheelbarrows, hedgehogs on their hind legs or mooning gnomes fall into this category; I couldn't possibly comment.

Abstract sculpture can work well in any style of garden, depending on the material and how the piece itself is displayed. A beautiful smooth crafted metal, wood or stone piece displayed on a simple plinth would work equally well in a traditional formal garden or a modern one. Something more free form, angular or organic would be better in an informal or modern setting. You can find modern sculpture in some garden centres, or in local art exhibitions.

If you cannot find exactly what you want, contact a local sculptor – through your nearest art college, perhaps – and commission a piece. Unless he or she is famous, it need not be prohibitively expensive and you will end up with a piece that suits your personality and your garden.

The positioning of any piece of sculpture is key. The temptation is to place it right in the middle of the garden, but in most cases, that would be a mistake. In a formal garden, a sculpture would look best against a simple background such as a hedge or a wall covered in evergreen climbers so that its contours stand out very clearly. In a more informal setting, sculpture is most effective among planting, where its solidity, smoothness and artifice contrast beautifully with the natural foliage around it. In Vita Sackville West's famous white garden at Sissinghurst, Kent, for example, a pale grey lead statue of a vestal virgin is placed under the canopy of a silver weeping pear.

Placing any sculptural object on a plinth immediately gives it much greater significance, turning it into a real work of art. Placing one on the ground gives a more informal effect, and can offer the pleasure of surprise.

ABOVE  The clean lines of a mirrored obelisk make a stunning contrast to the natural meadow planting around it.

OPPOSITE ABOVE  A collection of small disparate objects can work very well in a garden.

OPPOSITE BELOW LEFT  Three wooden spirals hanging from a tree have more impact than one..

OPPOSITE BELOW RIGHT  A large jar looks striking nestled in a border.

Of course, not everything that works well as a sculptural object was originally intended to be a piece of sculpture. Interesting found objects can often work very well in this context.

Natural materials can take on a strong sculptural look – pieces of driftwood, for example, bleached and worn by the sea. These look fantastic either in a natural setting, where they are part of nature and yet are also art or, even better in some ways, in a formal or modern one where the contrast between controlled artifice and free-form nature is strongest. The root systems of large fallen trees, carefully cleaned and even polished, often make very interesting, slightly sinister, organic shapes – like arthritic octopuses. Branches are similar, and with a minimal amount of trimming they can sometimes be made to resemble other things, like crocodiles or canoes, which can add an element of humour and surprise.

Jagged pieces of rock can be superbly sculptural and work very well in oriental-style or modern gardens. Place them on a patio or in a gravel garden. Lay them flat or stand them upright to resemble ancient standing stones. Large, smooth boulders can be used in similar ways, either on hard landscaping to contrast with the angular lines of the paving, or among planting where their solid smooth contours and the shapes and texture of the leaves enhance each other beautifully.

Manufactured objects, used in the right context, can also be very effective as garden sculpture. In a modern setting, a group of tall stainless-steel spirals, originally designed for supporting greenhouse tomatoes, look wonderful, as do long strips of thin solar panels, which move in the wind. They can also be wired to a battery to provide power for operating a water feature or some garden lighting, thereby adding function to form.

Lots of functional objects work well in this context. Old implements, for example, both horticultural and agricultural, are worth looking out for, though many, like old millstones, ploughs or watering cans now have antique status and a price tag to match. Stand them on a patio or in among planting. Industrial machine parts are another possibility, and many of them are surprisingly beautiful. Old grinding wheels or cogs look strikingly architectural on an old brick wall or even a modern rendered one. The very large ones – up to 80cm (32in) or more – are extremely dramatic but are very heavy, so you need to be sure that you place them where you need them first time. Stainless-steel engine parts, too, such as fans and casings, are worth looking out for, and ball bearings, which also come in a range of sizes, up to 1m (3ft) in diameter, are perfect stainless-steel spheres that would look stunning on the paving in a minimalist garden.

High-tech machine parts are also a possibility. Old computer disk drives, which are roughly the same size as pavers, could be used to make an interesting textured panel in among paving. CDs, of course, make great mobiles, hanging from trees and sending shafts of light darting all round the garden. They are also good for keeping the birds off edible crops, so they are functional, too.

ABOVE **A group of carefully spaced stones has an ancient, monolithic look. The play of light and shade on the flat planes adds interest.**

ABOVE CENTRE **Industrial salvage, like these rusting iron wheels attached to a weathered brick wall, can make great garden sculpture.**

ABOVE LEFT **Witty pink wooden tulips transform this area of unkempt grass.**

OPPOSITE LEFT **Metal spiral tomato supports make an elegant low-cost sculpture.**

OPPOSITE RIGHT **Small terracotta cane toppers are normally used to prevent injuries but in this vegetable plot they are purely decorative.**

## romantic containers

Terracotta works well in almost all gardens but is particularly good in informal or romantic settings. It is available in a range of styles, from plain machine-made flowerpots to highly decorated hand-thrown pots. Your choice will be dictated by taste and budget but especially if you are buying expensive terracotta, make sure it is guaranteed frost proof.

You can also buy very good plastic imitation terracotta pots, which look almost like the real thing. They have the advantage of being lightweight and unbreakable, although they do not age in the same way. They can look extremely stylish with a paint effect – there are easy-to-use kits for verdigris, pewter or rusting iron-finish – as long as you use an acrylic undercoat and seal them with waterproof varnish.

There are very good relatively inexpensive frost-proof ceramic pots available now. Among the most attractive are the plain Chinese cloud pots in rich dark blue or a lighter turquoise glaze. You can also find ceramic pots painted with bamboo designs or Chinese calligraphy, which would be fine in an oriental-style garden but might look a little out of keeping in a cottage garden. Large rough and chunky glazed brown Thai water butts add a striking sculptural element, planted or unplanted.

Wood is another good material for containers in romantic informal gardens, particularly in the form of half barrels or square rough-sawn tubs.

Baskets woven from willow also make terrific containers if you treat them with several coats of coloured wood stain or waterproof yacht varnish first and line them with stout black polythene before you plant. They will not last forever but will give you a lot of container for your money for a few years.

When it comes to planting in formal and romantic containers, a useful rule of thumb is that the more elaborate the container the simpler the display needs to be and vice versa. So a very ornately decorated pot will look stunning with just one type of plant – trailing scarlet pelargoniums, perhaps, or blue-leafed hostas – while a plain wooden half barrel needs a more interesting combination of shapes and colours.

In either case, the most attractive containers are those that are packed with plants. You don't want to see any bare compost, and in the case of a simple container, you don't want to see a great deal of the container, either. Choose plants of different habits – some trailing to soften the edges, some upright to add height to the display, others bushy to fill in.

Think about colour themes, too. In a very small area like a container, a limited range of colours works best: too many colours in close proximity cancel each other out. Red, white and blue is always popular with traditional gardeners, while for a romantic garden, pastels such as pink, mauve, pale blue and white along with silver foliage look terrific. Single-colour planting can look stunning. Yellow, for example, ranges from deep cream through lemon, butter and apricot to deep gold. White is always very elegant. With this colour, the interest comes from the contrasting flower shapes and sizes – try tiny white lobelia or gypsophila, with larger busy lizzies and big blowsy double begonias – together with the different greens of the foliage.

ABOVE **A motley collection of containers is linked by the planting style – architectural and mainly evergreen. The plain white walls also lend cohesion.**

LEFT **Container planting can be just as valuable in winter. This group of grasses and purple-leafed *Heuchera* looks good rimed with frost.**

OPPOSITE **Baskets make great low-cost planters for a romantic setting if you weatherproof them with yacht varnish. Where the material and the planting are identical, it adds interest to use slightly differently shaped baskets.**

**romantic containers / 97**

Formal containers can be made from the same materials as those for informal gardens, but what makes the difference is not only the shape and the planting but also the positioning. A pair of identical containers either side of a front door or a bench, for example, immediately adds a degree of formality, as would four matching containers at the corners of a square or rectangular pool.

Formal containers are usually on a grander scale than informal ones. Large stone urns, for example, look marvellous in large gardens – evoking the great classical gardens of Italy and France – but they can also be stunning in very small city gardens where their disproportionate scale is very dramatic and exciting. The genuine article can cost as much as a second-hand car, but reproduction urns of reconstituted stone are cheaper, and concrete replicas are cheapest of all. The latter do look very stark and new, but can be easily 'distressed' with a hammer and chisel, and a coat of well-watered down dark brown emulsion to age them. If you can be a little less impatient, painting them with plain yoghurt or sour milk, or even liquid manure. quickly encourages algae and lichen to grow on them, adding a welcome patina of age.

Terracotta can also be used to make formal containers, as long as the shape is right. Simple shapes such as cubes, straight-sided cylinders and old flower-pot shapes look best in formal settings, with any pattern kept to a minimum.

Wood is an excellent material for this style of garden, but here it is used in a sophisticated way, planed and painted rather than left rough-hewn. The square Versailles tub is the best-known example of a formal container, with its panelled sides and round knobs at each corner. Versailles tubs can be painted any colour, although black, white or dark green are the most usual choice. Wood obviously requires regular maintenance, but there are now some very good imitations available that need little looking after. These are plastic or fibreglass and the best are made from moulds of the genuine article, so that the wood grain looks extremely convincing even close up.

Metal, too, makes good formal containers. Square or rectangular lead tanks work well in traditional settings, although the reproduction versions made from fibreglass are totally convincing, much lighter in weight and carry no health risk. Other metals such as copper, aluminium, stainless steel and galvanized metal in strong, simple geometric shapes also look very good in a modern formal garden.

Planting in formal containers needs to be simpler on the whole. Architectural plants – those with very large boldly shaped leaves – are ideally suited to formality because they reinforce the simple geometry of the containers themselves. Spiky evergreen cordylines, phormiums or large-leafed hostas are all very good choices.

Topiary – small-leaved evergreen shrubs such as box, euonymus or holly clipped into geometric shapes – is also an excellent choice. All you need in a container is, say, a single box ball or lollipop, spiral or pyramid to make an immediate impact in the garden.

Topiary, especially made from box, takes careful training over a number of years, so you will find that it is expensive to buy. As a less expensive alternative, stand an obelisk made of trellis or wire in your container. This will create that sharp architectural outline right away, then you can grow a fast-growing plant such as a small-leaved plain green ivy over it. If you keep it well clipped, the outline will remain crisp and the angles sharp.

RIGHT **A row of identical containers with matching planting always has great impact. Spiky variegated agaves in lined-up galvanized buckets are modern yet formal.**

OPPOSITE **Lavenders grown in terracotta half-pots have a soft traditional feel, while still looking formal.**

## modern containers

In contemporary gardens, containers can be used either sculpturally, with perhaps one large striking container with an equally striking plant, or formally. Try rows of small square 'lead' tanks, planted with mind-your-own-business (*Soleirolia soleirolii*). Metal is an ideal material for modern garden containers. Bright shiny aluminium and stainless steel or less reflective copper and galvanized metal are all wonderful choices, especially if the containers are in simple strong angular shapes such as cubes or cylinders.

Glass containers are another good choice, provided the glass is thick and toughened. Try using glass for growing plants like the tall papyrus (*Cyperus papyrus*) hydroponically, in layers of coloured gravel or bright plastic chippings and water. If you want to grow plants in the normal way in glass, you will need drainage holes in the bottom of the container – get a professional to make them for you. Alternatively, use glass to hold brightly coloured canes or dried stems. This is ideal for a spot where there is virtually no light, such as under a stairwell.

Unashamed plastic, not pretending to be anything but itself, is also an exciting modern material. Look in homeware or office stores rather than garden centres for brightly coloured containers in bold simple shapes. Again, you will need to make drainage holes in them. Pearlized plastic footballs make very striking containers if you slice the top off and pack firmly with compost.

In a modern garden terracotta also plays a part, only this time in the form of inexpensive machine-made pots painted in bright colours. There exists paint specially formulated for this purpose, but the colour range is limited, so use any outdoor acrylic paint. Be bold with colour. Hot shades – magenta, orange, lime green – are effective planted with a single cool shade – white for example, or blue. Black is also very striking, especially with other pots sprayed silver and planted with silvery or black foliage. If you are artistic, paint on patterns in contrasting colours, either freehand or with the help of stencils. Simple circles, triangles or stars are more effective in this context than flowers or bows.

As for planting, again, clean strong shapes work well. Spiky phormiums, cordylines and silvery astelias are good, as are ornamental grasses. The beautiful evergreen pheasant's tail grass (*Stipa arundinacea*) or the steel blue *Helictotrichon sempervirens* would be striking all year round, while on a smaller scale, three or four plants of blue fescue (*Festuca glauca*) or the black *Ophiopogon planiscapus* 'Nigrescens' in a galvanized window box would make a stylish minimalist display. With modern containers you don't need to cover the compost entirely with planting, so try top dressing with crushed glass, metal granules or flakes of smoky purple slate. Any of these will add to the strong modern feel you are creating.

ABOVE  Brightly painted oil drums offer a lot of growing space.

ABOVE LEFT  The agave with its slate mulch looks very modern and stylish. Growing it in a pot means it can easily be taken inside in winter.

OPPOSITE LEFT
Metal pipes of different heights make an unusual containerized herb and vegetable garden. The plants are grown in pots which are slotted into the top of each pipe.

OPPOSITE RIGHT  A simple shallow china bowl with a hole in the base for drainage shows off the startling foliage of Japanese blood grass (*Imperata cylindrica* 'Red Baron') to perfection.

# potted jungle

**YOU WILL NEED**

- 1 x black fibreglass container,
  60 x 60 x 40cm (24 x 24 x 16 in)
- 2 x black fibreglass containers,
  40 x 40 x 40cm (16 x 16 x 16in)
- 2 x black fibreglass containers,
  30 x 30 x 30cm (1 x 1 x 1ft)
- 1 x *Phyllostachys nigra*
- 1 x *Fatsia japonica*
- 1 x *Strelitzia reginae*
- 3 x *Canna* 'Durban'
- 3 x *Carex flagellifera*
- 12 x *Bacopa* 'Snowflake'

## zebra stripes • wild colour

The dark green diagonal fence around this roof terrace was visually very dominant, so the first thing we did was to paint it and the low brick wall beneath it in a pale sage green. It immediately blended into the background and made you much more aware of the large trees beyond.

To create a jungle look, we chose plants primarily for their foliage, some exotic and tender, like the brilliant red-and-green striped canna, *Canna* 'Durban', and the bird of paradise, *Strelitzia reginae*, with its elegant blue-green, paddle-shaped evergreen leaves. These two also flower, the bird of paradise producing in early summer bright orange flowers that do look astonishingly bird-like, and the canna producing spikes of hot orange flowers in late summer. They are not reliably hardy though, and while cannas may survive with some protection outside in a sheltered position, the bird of paradise needs to over-winter inside in a frost-free place.

The other plants look exotic but are in fact hardy, like *Fatsia japonica*, with its large glossy evergreen hand-shaped leaves and golf-ball-like heads of flowers in autumn that turn into black berries in winter. For height, and sound when the wind is rustling through its canes, we chose the stylish black-stemmed bamboo, *Phyllostachys nigra*. When they appear, the new canes are sea-green, but after the first season they acquire their distinctive glossy black colour. For instant impact, you should buy a large plant, although *Phyllostachys* is very fast-growing and will put on 3m (10ft) of growth in just a few weeks.

We also planted the evergreen sedge, *Carex flagellifera*, which is a rich coppery colour and has very attractive arching flowers and seedheads in pale golden brown. To make an interesting underplanting, we used *Bacopa* (sometimes called *Sutera*) 'Snowflake', a creeping annual with neat green leaves and attractive small white flowers.

Since weight is a consideration on a roof terrace, we used light but very strong square fibreglass containers (as well as light soil-less compost) with drainage holes drilled in the bottom. Black is the ideal colour because it tends to disappear and does not compete with the planting. To prevent the containers drying out too quickly, we mixed water-retaining gel crystals into the compost as we planted.

# herbal chequerboard

### YOU WILL NEED

- 5 x square metal containers 30 x 30 x 30cm (1 x 1 x 1ft)
- 1 x 2-litre pot (3¹/₂-pint) *Rosmarinus* 'Miss Jessopp's Upright')
- 1 x 2-litre pot (3¹/₂-pint) (or 4 x 9-cm [3¹/₂-in] pots) *Salvia officinalis* 'Purpurascens')
- 1 x 2-litre pot (3¹/₂-pint) (or 4 x 9-cm [3¹/₂-in] pots) mint
- 1 x 2-litre pot (3¹/₂-pint) (or 4 x 9-cm [3¹/₂-in] pots) chives
- 1 x 2-litre pot (3¹/₂-pint) (or 4 x 9-cm [3¹/₂-in] pots) *Foeniculum vulgare* 'Purpureum')
- 4 x 9-cm [3¹/₂-in] pots thyme (to underplant the rosemary)
- soil-based compost
- approximately 4.5m (15ft) of 5 x 25cm (2 x 1in) timber
- 4 x 'L' brackets
- black gloss paint for exterior use
- decorative mulch

## a feast for the eye

A herb garden like this is perfect for the impatient gardener who also loves to cook because it can be used – judiciously – from day one.

With so many herbs available now, your choice depends on what you most like to use and what will best suit the conditions you have. For example, mint likes some shade, while Mediterranean herbs such as thyme and rosemary need sun. And since this herb garden should be decorative as well as functional, choose herbs that look good. Instead of plain green sage or fennel, go for the purple-leaved varieties – *Salvia officinalis* 'Purpurascens' and *Foeniculum vulgare* 'Purpureum' respectively. There are also many pretty variegated thymes. All of these varieties have the same intensity of flavour as their plain relatives.

For winter interest, choose some evergreen herbs such as rosemary, thyme and sage. Mint, chives and fennel are perennial plants, which will die down in autumn but come up again next spring, while other herbs, like basil, are annuals and need to be replaced every year.

Since this is a permanent planting and weight is not a factor, use a free-draining, soil-based compost. For our modern herb garden, we chose plain metal cube-shaped containers. To add a degree of formality, we arranged them in a chequerboard pattern and surrounded them with a simple wooden frame painted black. This was made from 5 x 2.5cm (2 x 1in) timber, joined at the corners with simple metal 'L' brackets.

In between the containers, we laid a mulch made of crushed CDs. These add texture and their silvery sparkle picks up the metal of the containers. You could also use industrial aluminium off-cuts, crushed or water-washed glass in a range of colours, or small pebbles or crushed shells stained in vibrant shades such as purple, electric blue or bright yellow.

the soft touches

# quick fixes with plants

**W**hatever the state of the garden you have taken on, some plants offer quick-fix solutions that are perfect for the impatient gardener. In overgrown gardens they can provide focus and diversion (see pages 24–25) amid the chaos and in virgin plots, annuals, either grown from seed *in situ* or planted out as bedding plants, can do a great job in a very short time.

## solutions using climbers

ABOVE **Sweet peas, bought as small plants from the garden centre, provide a temporary riot of colour and fragrance against a dull hedge in just a few weeks.**

**I**f your garden is not a wilderness but just is not as exciting as you might like, you can very easily improve on what is there for some near-instant gratification. If you have mature shrubs that are either evergreen or flower only briefly in say winter, spring or early summer, use them as a framework for colourful climbers. Many of the small-flowered species clematis are perfect for this purpose because they are not too vigorous, flower freely for a long period and can be cut back when flowering is over. For flowers from midsummer right through until autumn, look for clematis cultivars such as the wine-red *Clematis* 'Madame Julia Correvon', the green-and-white *C.* 'Alba Luxurians', the pale lilac-blue *C.* 'Betty Corning' or the pink *C.* 'Princess Diana'. One of the very best is the double *C. viticella* 'Purpurea Plena Elegans', which has beautiful fluffy flowers in soft purple, reminscent of the colour of faded velvet.

Texensis hybrids, which flower at the same time, are also lovely, with their tulip-shaped flowers in rich pink (*Clematis* 'Duchess of Albany') or rich red (*C.* 'Gravetye Beauty'). Both of these species are especially useful because their dead growth needs to be cut back to the first leaf joints above the ground in winter, leaving the host shrub unencumbered when it is giving its own display.

You could also grow clematis over a dull hedge – a species such as *C. flammula* with its almond-scented, small starry white flowers in late summer would be a good choice because it looks a little like the native old man's beard (*C. vitalba*), which grows in hedgerows. Over a conifer hedge, you could try the brilliant scarlet flame creeper (*Tropaeolum speciosum*), which is one of those temperamental plants that only grows where the conditions suit it perfectly. It demands a rich deep moist soil, with its head in the sun and its roots in cool

shade. But it is really spectacular so it is well worth having it in the garden.

Annual climbers are another good quick fix choice because they are both fast and temporary. You could try sweet peas. These will happily scramble through existing shrubs though you need to pick the flowers regularly to keep the plants producing more – not that this is a hardship. The taller varieties of nasturtiums (*Tropaeolum majus*) are good for growing up hedges – they prefer the rather poor soil that you find at the base of a hedge to more fertile soil, which results in masses of leaves, but not many flowers. Canary creeper (*Tropaeolum perigrinum*), a delightful relation, has fluffy bright yellow flowers reminiscent of Woodstock in the Peanuts cartoons, and bright green feathery foliage. The twining snapdragon (*Maurandya* 'Victoria Falls') has vibrant cerise-purple trumpets from early summer to the first frosts.

ABOVE **Enjoying perfect conditions, the aptly named Flame Creeper (***Tropaeolum speciosum***) scrambles happily over a yew hedge.**

LEFT **Small-flowered varieties of clematis such as *C. texensis* 'Gravetye Beauty' are ideal for quick fixes – fast growing but since they are cut back each year, not ungovernable.**

**solutions using climbers / 111**

# solutions using annuals

**YOU WILL NEED:**
- 2 x packets *Papaver commutatum* 'Ladybird' seed
- 1 x packet *Hordeum jubatum* seed
- 3 x plastic spirals
- 3 x 30cm (1ft) wooden stakes of 2.5 x 2.5cm (1 x 1in) timber

## poppies and spirals

Hardy annuals, which are sown directly into the soil where they are to flower, are a great way of creating a splash of colour in the garden in the first summer. They don't cost a fortune nor do they compromise anything you may want to do in the longer term. You can sow as small or as large an area as you like – a border or even a whole garden.

Although you can sow a mixture of annuals, the greatest impact comes from using a mass of one or two varieties. We chose the delightful annual poppy, *Papaver commutatum* 'Ladybird', which has attractive scalloped fern-like leaves and bright red flowers with a distinctive black spot on each petal. Through the area, we also sowed a ribbon of the very attractive annual squirrel-tail grass, *Hordeum jubatum*.

As a modern sculptural finishing touch, we used three brightly coloured plastic spirals – one red, two orange. These were wedged into grooves sawn in the top of short wooden stakes, which were then pushed into the soil among the planting so the stakes would not show. The spirals are flexible so they move attractively in the wind. If you cannot find exactly the same spirals, you could use a group of stainless-steel spiral tomato supports or even slender poles of different heights painted in bands of bright colour.

Sow the seeds in late spring into prepared soil, that is to say, dug over, weeded and raked roughly level. In the unlikely event of the weather being dry at that time of year, water the soil a few hours before you plan to sow. If you sow too early, especially in cold wet grey weather, the seeds will simply not germinate at all or will struggle to germinate.

Poppy seeds are very fine – one seed packet contains several hundred – so mix them with some

silver sand to make them easier to sow. Sow thinly to minimize the need for thinning out when the seeds germinate. As for the ribbon of grasses, scratch a wavy line through the planting area and sow the grass seed in that.

When the seeds germinate, you must thin out the seedlings if you are to have strong sturdy plants. The final spacing for the poppies should be about 20cm (8in) and for the grass about 15cm (6in).

If you are too late to grow from seed, you could achieve a similar effect with annual plants from the garden centre, but this will be much more expensive and you may not find exactly the varieties you want.

ABOVE  The silver leaves of *Artemisia stelleriana* 'Silver Brocade' syn. 'Boughton Silver' combine well with the lime-green foliage and magenta flowers of *Geranium* 'Ann Folkard' scrambling through it.

ABOVE RIGHT  Blue love-in-a-mist (*Nigella*) sown informally among the spiky silver *Eryngium* x *oliverianum* is an ideal filler in the first year while the eryngium gets established.

OPPOSITE  A dull, neglected rose border was given a facelift in a single season simply by pruning the roses hard to encourage healthy new growth and weaving a dozen grasses – *Calamagrostis* x *acutiflora* 'Overdam' – among them.

Your inherited garden may well feature mixed borders that have a few shrubs as backbone and lots of perennials. What has often happened is that the border has been planted ad hoc, without a great deal of thought and with lots of impulse buys, so that the overall effect is bitty and unsatisfying.

But it is not necessary to dig everything up and start again in order to make it look a lot better. One way to give it a satisfying unity is to repeat one type of plant in bold groups throughout. You will probably need a group roughly at either end and one or more in the middle, depending on the size of the border. Obviously the groups should not be in a straight line or in too regular a pattern.

Alternatively, weave a ribbon of these plants right through the border. Use canes to mark the desired positions, and when everything looks right, dig out any plants that are in the way and either replant them elsewhere or give them away.

In a sunny border that lacks height, an ideal plant would be *Verbena bonariensis*. This grows up to 2m (6ft 6in) high, with small clusters of intense purple flowers on stiff slender angular stems. It has such an open and airy habit that it works just as well right at the front of a border as it does at the back. It is semi-evergreen and even when the flowers have died and turned russet, it adds useful structure to the winter scene. Russian sage (*Perovskia* 'Blue Spire) would be another good choice here. It is not quite as tall – about 1.2m (4ft) – but has almost white felty stems, silvery leaves and spikes of small lavender-blue flowers.

Silver foliage plants are useful for a quick fix as they work just as well with pastel shades as they do with 'hot' ones. *Artemisa* 'Powis Castle', with very finely divided foliage, is a good choice to repeat, while *Helichrysum petiolare* is good to weave through. This is usually grown in hanging baskets, producing long trails over 1m (3ft 3in) in length, but it will do very well scrambling through a border, literally weaving it all together. Some hardy geraniums do the same job.

*Geranium wallichianum* 'Buxton's Variety' syn. *G.* 'Buxton's Blue' for instance, has pretty blue flowers with a white eye that last from late summer until well into the autumn, while *G.* 'Ann Folkard', which has lime-green leaves and magenta flowers (a combination which, surprisingly, works very well) will scramble for up to 1.2m (4ft).

You can also use hardy annuals to weave through existing planting to great effect – one packet of good old blue love-in-a-mist (*Nigella*) or the white corn cockle (*Agrostemma githago* 'Ocean Pearl') sown in waves through the border is all you need. If it is too late to sow, buy taller annuals such as cosmos or tobacco plants from the garden centre.

A tall, upright grass such as *Calamagrostis* would work well in groups, while the smaller fine *Stipa tenuissima* could be woven right through a border, giving the other plants a context.

In a shady border, leathery evergreen bergenias would make substantial groups, as would evergreen ferns such as *Polystichum setiferum* or small shrubs like variegated *Euonymus fortunei* 'Emerald Gaiety'. For height, try Japanese anemones like the white *Anemone* x *hybrida* 'Honorine Jobert' or the rich pink *A.* x *h.* 'Queen Charlotte' (syn. *A.* x *h.* 'Königin Charlotte'), which flower from midsummer to autumn.

## phased planting

As an impatient gardener, you clearly want results quickly, and if you are prepared to spend the money, you can have an instant garden, either using predominantly annuals or buying in large mature plants. Taking the annuals route is fine; you will have lots of colour in summer, but of course everything will die off in the autumn and you'll have to plant it all again for next year's show. Buying very large mature plants is an excellent way of getting instant maturity, but filling the whole garden this way will cost an absolute fortune and in many instances, smaller plants will get established far better and will soon catch up. But I'm not suggesting that you revert to old-fashioned methods of planting very small shrubs at the correct distance apart and waiting five years for anything approaching a good show. What I am suggesting is

that you go in for phased planting, which will give you the best of both worlds.

To make phased planting easy, I have divided plants into Fast, Medium and Slow categories. Fast are those that will give you a good show in their first season, filling the space without getting out of control, but on the whole they are not plants you will keep for more than one or two years. Excluded from this category are thugs like Russian vine, which are very fast, but do not know when to stop. I don't even have to mention Leyland cypress, do I? These monster conifers have had so much adverse publicity of late that you wouldn't even consider planting them as a hedge.

Medium plants are those that are a little slower to get going, but will start to perform well in their second and third seasons. Slow plants are those that will not

ABOVE **Behind a collection of young Japanese maples and cordylines in pots, which will eventually form a denser screen, the box-edged bed contains alliums for an early summer display.**

reach their full potential for many years, although in the meantime they will still make a valuable contribution to the garden. In fact some Slow plants are invaluable for the impatient gardener, especially one with limited space, or one who moves frequently. A plant such as a Japanese maple or a variegated pittosporum, which is very slow growing, looks great from the day you buy it, and will stay happily in a small bed or a container for many years.

The joy of phased planting is that you do the bulk of the work now – and the same work is involved whether you are planting a fast temporary plant or a slow permanent one – but you will carry on getting the rewards for years to come without much additional effort. All you will need to do in subsequent years is remove the odd Fast plant that has served its purpose,

and some tweaking – deadheading, cutting back dead growth in the autumn, maybe eventually dividing up large clumps of perennials.

When you are choosing plants from the three categories, you need to think about conditions and make sure those you choose all like the same sort of soil and the same amount of sun or shade. Think about colour schemes, too. In small spaces, you need to use colour with care, limiting yourself to just a few. By all means go for strong, bright colours – reds, oranges, yellows – but do so full-bloodedly and don't mix in pale pastel shades as well. If you have room, use those in a different part of the garden, or use colour seasonally. For early summer, for example, go for soft blues, pinks and mauves, but for late summer/early autumn, choose plants with rich red or gold flowers or foliage.

ABOVE **The same bed as shown opposite less than four months later is transformed by huge annual castor oil plants (*Ricinus*) planted out in late spring and the tender blue-grey perennial *Melianthus major*.**

# phased planting in sun

## YOU WILL NEED

- 1 x *Clematis* 'Prince Charles'
- 1 x *Pittosporum* 'Silver Queen'
- 1 x *Rosa* 'Mary Rose'
- 3 x *Lavandula angustifolia* 'Hidcote'
- 1 x *Cynara cardunculus*
- 6 x blue *Lathyrus odoratus*
- 3 x *Ipomoea indica*
- 1 x packet *Nigella damascena* 'Miss Jekyll'
- opaque wood treatment in light grey

## symphony in mauve and pink

Our sunny border was bounded on three sides by a fence, a trellis screen and, half way down the long narrow garden, an arch. The trellis was originally a deep rusty brown colour so to flatter the colours of our pink, blue and silver planting scheme, we painted it with an opaque wood treatment in light grey. The bed was about 2.2m (7ft) long and only about 45cm (18in) deep – not deep enough to grow decent sized shrubs, so we almost doubled the depth by removing a strip of lawn.

The Slow plant we chose is *Pittosporum* 'Silver Queen'. This is an attractive evergreen shrub, forming a neat conical shape, with grey-green leaves that are so heavily speckled with silvery white that the overall appearance is of silver. It isn't reliably hardy everywhere so in colder gardens you might find that a variegated holly (*Ilex aquifolium* 'Silver Queen') would be a safer bet. The holly is very slow growing, reaching 10m (30ft) in twenty years or so, but in the unlikely event that you stay put that long, you can perfectly easily keep it clipped.

Among the Medium plants is *Clematis* 'Prince Charles', growing up the trellis at the back. This has very attractive small flowers in a soft lavender blue, borne in profusion from midsummer to well into the autumn. If the plant you buy only has one or two stems, cut them down to just above the lowest pair of buds or leaves. This will go against the grain – how can chopping a plant right back produce results quickly? What it will do is encourage it to produce more shoots from the base, resulting in quicker, denser coverage, and since this is a clematis that flowers on growth it

makes in the current season you will still get a show of flowers in the first summer.

The Medium shrub here is an English rose, *R.* 'Mary Rose'. This forms a dense bush, eventually reaching 1.2m x 1m (4ft x 3ft 3in), with a succession of fragrant double rose-pink flowers for months during summer and early autumn.

As for Fast plants, some of these are more temporary than others. Lavender – we used the reliable *L. angustifolia* 'Hidcote' – gives a good show in its first year, with silvery green leaves and spikes of dark purple flowers. Provided it is clipped over each spring to stop it getting leggy, it will last a good few years before it needs replacing. Plant a group of three for impact.

The temporary star of our sunny border is a cardoon, which reaches well over 2m (6½ft) in height. It has long, jagged silvery leaves up to 1m (3ft 3in) in length and intense purple thistle flowers. It will die down in autumn, and come back next year, but by then it will have served its purpose in this border, so you can take it out.

As fillers in the first season, hardy annuals are invaluable. Love-in-a-mist (*Nigella damascena* 'Miss Jekyll') is an ideal choice with its very fine feathery bright green foliage weaving through the permanent plants. It produces jewel-like rich blue flowers, followed by equally attractive seed heads. As fillers on the trellis, we planted sweet peas in shades of blue, and rich purple morning glories bought as young plants from a garden centre and planted out after all danger of frost had passed.

## phased planting in shade

ABOVE **A shady border includes wine-red** *Cotinus* **'Grace', fresh green hardy geraniums and variegated** *Hosta* **'Francee'.**

ABOVE RIGHT *Geranium macrorrhizum* **'Bevan's Variety' is ideal for dry shade under trees.**

OPPOSITE LEFT **The hart's tongue fern (***Asplenium scolopendrium***) makes attractive ground cover.**

OPPOSITE RIGHT *Impatiens* **New Guinea hybrids add colour to mainly green planting schemes in shade.**

Many town and city gardens have to contend with shade from surrounding buildings or trees, but far from being a problem, this can be an opportunity to create a cool green space. And since there's no point fighting nature, it means using plants that enjoy shade, which on the whole are foliage plants.

You may think that so much green together is boring, but if you choose contrasting leaf shapes and textures, along with different shades of green, you can have planting schemes that are full of interest and last longer than many schemes that rely largely on flowers.

On the wall or fence, choose a Slow plant like the large-leafed Persian ivy (*Hedera colchica* 'Variegata'). This has cool grey-green and cream variegations, adding lightness, but since it takes a few seasons to get going, also plant a Fast golden hop (*Humulus lupulus* 'Aureus') to give you a show in the first year or so. Plant it at the far end of the border, so that it will not crowd the ivy. The hop will be more lime green than gold in shade, but it will be a useful temporary space-filler and can be dug out when the ivy is growing well.

Evergreen shrubs will make up the framework of this shady border and under the Medium heading, *Fatsia japonica* is an excellent choice. It has large hand-shaped leaves whose glossy surface helps bounce the light around in a shady spot, as well as curious white golf-ball-like flowers that turn to black berries. Although it looks exotic and adds a jungly feel to a border, it is very hardy. The Mexican Orange Blossom (*Choisya ternata*) is another very good structural evergreen, especially the finer-leaved *C.* 'Aztec Pearl'. It forms a neat rounded shape, and has large white flowers in late spring or early summer and often again in autumn. White flowers are ideal in shade because they show up more clearly than darker colours.

Among the perennials, *Acanthus mollis* with its big jagged leaves and spikes of white and purple hooded flowers makes a bold statement. So does the hellebore, *H. argutifolius* with apple-green flowers in late winter or early spring and jagged leathery green leaves that survive the winter, but are best removed when the new leaves appear.

Ferns enjoy shady conditions and so are a great choice as Medium plants, especially evergreen ferns such as the finely divided *Polystichum setiferum* Divisilobum Group, or the hart's tongue fern (*Asplenium scolopendrium*).

In the first season, you will also need a few Fast plants to fill in the gaps in your garden. The hardy geranium, *Geranium macrorrhizum*, is one of the best ground-cover plants for shade, and especially where there is dry shade. It forms dense, weed-proof mats about 30cm (1ft) high of aromatic soft evergreen leaves and has sprays of white, pink or magenta flowers in spring. Woodruff (*Galium odoratum*) is a lovely low carpeting plant for shady conditions, with pretty scalloped leaves and small white starry flowers in spring and summer.

There are comparatively few bedding plants that like shade, but luckily one of those that do is busy lizzie (*Impatiens*). In white, pale pink or apricot, it really stands out, while the vivid scarlet, orange or magenta of the large New Guinea hybrids add a tropical feel.

LEFT **A simple terracotta urn planted with trailing** *Lotus bertholottii* **makes a superb focal point. The surrounding planting is of** *Perovskia, Convolvulus cneorum,* **thyme, purple sage and catmint.**

## phased planting in a gravel garden

Gravel gardens are ideal for impatient gardeners because, even though the plants are small, the expanse of gravel is part of the look in a way that bare soil would not be in an ordinary border, so it looks good right from the start. That's not to say, of course that it won't look even better in a few years once the plants have really established themselves and spread.

Architectural plants work well in this context, so for a Slow plant, a spiky cordyline would be a good choice. If budget permits you could buy a large mature plant for instant effect, but if not, a small plant will look still good and after three or four years will catch up. Yuccas are also a good choice here, though their very sharp pointed leaves mean they should be sited with some care. Silver-leaved plants also work well in this context, and for large background shrubs, try *Elaeagnus* 'Quicksilver', with elegant leaves that keep their bright silver colour right through until the autumn.

There are very good silver-leaved plants in the Medium category, too. The relatively low-growing shrub, *Convolvulus cneorum* is an excellent choice; it is evergreen with small, slender, spoon-shaped leaves that have a pearly sheen, and typical convolvulus trumpet flowers that open white from tightly furled pink-tinged buds. Lambs' ears (*Stachys byzantina*), with its furry grey leaves, is another good choice, forming soft mounds of foliage. It has yellow flowers, but if you dislike the colour, snip them off and be rewarded with fresh new leaves. Purple sage is a great contrast to silver foliage. Both may look a little battered after the winter, so cut them back in spring. Picking up the spiky theme, *Sisyrinchium striatum* 'Variegatum' is a good choice, forming neat clumps of pale green and cream variegated leaves with spikes of neat round white flowers in summer. It seeds itself freely – perhaps too freely – but in gravel the seedlings are easily removed.

As for the Fast plants, *Verbascum olympicum* produces a large rosette of grey felted leaves the first year and tall stems of bright yellow flowers opening from bright silvery grey buds the next. Try to buy one-year-old plants to get the full benefit in the first year. These are temporary stars, though, and will usually die after they have flowered. If not, remove them when they compete with the permanent plants for space.

Russian sage (*Perovskia*) is a great permanent perennial, producing tall spikes of soft lavender-blue flowers on almost white stems, with slim, jagged grey leaves. It reaches virtually its full height in the first season, but will then spread to form a significant clump in subsequent years. Cut it back hard each spring as the new growth appears. Catmint (*Nepeta* x *faassenii*) is invaluable for the softening effect it has, forming drifts of grey-green leaves and producing hazy blue-mauve flowers. Clip it over once it has flowered to keep it neat. A very useful Fast plant for gravel gardens is one that is usually grown in hanging baskets – *Helichrysum petiolare*. In hanging baskets, its long trails of round, felted grey leaves hang down, but grown in the ground, these scramble along the surface of the soil and through other plants. For instant colour in a gravel garden in the first season, California poppies (*Eschscholzia californica*) in shades of hot orange and red or paler pinks and creams are hard to beat. They will self-seed in subsequent years, though as the permanent plants expand and cover the ground they will gradually die out.

OPPOSITE **Spiky variegated sisyrinchiums work well against a background of gravel, while purple osteospermums add a splash of temporary summer colour.**

A jungle garden is ideal for impatient gardeners because it can be achieved relatively quickly. The secret in temperate climates is to use a mixture of exotic plants that are hardy enough to survive in a sheltered garden and hardy plants that have a jungly look. This type of garden can be virtually instant if you buy very large tree ferns (*Dicksonia antarctica*), hardy palms (*Trachycarpus fortunei*) and phormiums, but even if you buy plants of a reasonable size it doesn't take many years to achieve the same effect.

Growing about 2.5cm (1in) a year, tree ferns are undoubtedly Slow but even a relatively small one will have great impact. If you buy a smaller specimen, put it in a large pot to add to its height. Surround it with planting and the pot will never show. The Chusan palm (*Trachycarpus fortunei*) may be slow to get going, but once it does, it grows quickly.

As for Medium plants, phormiums (*Phormium tenax*) are a good choice. They have sword-like leaves and, when older, curious spikes of rusty-red flowers. For sheer stature, the plain green or bronze-leaved varieties are hard to beat. *Fatsia japonica* looks like a jungle plant but is hardy in all but the coldest gardens, while for a simpler, less attention-seeking filler, evergreen *Viburnum tinus* is ideal. A few splashes of bright colour are welcome in the jungle. A purple rhododendron does the job in late spring, while acer foliage follows through to the autumn.

Fast plants add still more drama. Ornamental rhubarb (*Rheum palmatum*) is a wonderful space-filler, producing huge jagged leaves in the first season along with tall spikes of fluffy pink flowers, which turn rusty brown as they fade. *Acanthus spinosus* is also great for a jungly look, producing spires of hooded purple and white flowers in summer. A multiple planting of the latter two will give a great jungle look in the first season, but as the other plants grow, thin them out. Hardy ferns such as aspleniums and polypodiums are good space fillers, while for a splash of short-term colour go for a mass of New Guinea hybrid busy lizzies, with flowers in vibrant, almost luminous shades of magenta, scarlet, pink and orange.

RIGHT **The simple brick-edged lawn is the ideal foil for the complex tapestry of jungle foliage surrounding it. This style of planting creates a restful, private space very quickly.**

These are plants that will give a very good show in their first season, in most cases putting on plenty of height – important in creating impact in a new garden or border – but which won't get out of control. Some are shrubs that are used as temporary fillers and can either be taken out in the second or third season, once the permanent planting has begun to fill out. Others are varieties that thrive on being cut back hard each year, which keeps them more or less the same size. Others are herbaceous perennials, which means they die down every autumn, and will grow again the following spring, so that they are limited in height to the amount of growth they can make in one season. Some will be only temporary stars, to be removed once the other plants have reached a decent size, while others can be permanent features of the border. Obviously the size of a plant after one season depends to a large extent on the size it is when you buy it; I am assuming that you buy the largest available in the average garden centre.

Measurements are given for each plant's growth. Height is followed by spread.

## fast plants

★ *Temporary Star*
▲ *Stayer*

## CLIMBERS

*Climbers are invaluable for the impatient gardener in a number of ways. Grown up obelisks or wigwams they can give height in a newly planted area far more quickly than any other plants, and they can brighten up walls and fences, too. They are also invaluable for adding interest to existing shrubs or hedges that are serviceable but dull. The following are examples of useful climbers that will give a good show even in the first year that you plant them.*

Cardoon (*Cynara cardunculus*)

## ▲ Clematis armandii

SIZE AFTER ONE SEASON: 1.8 x 1.8m (6 x 6ft)
ULTIMATE SIZE: 7.5 x 7.5m (25 x 25ft)
This evergreen clematis is a handsome plant for a town garden, producing long slender leathery leaves and masses of white (*C. a.* 'Snowdrift') or blush-white (*C. a.* 'Apple Blossom') flowers in spring, which are also scented. It is good trained up and along the top of a wall or allowed to scramble through an old tree. Although it is hardy down to −15°C (5°F), it does best with some protection from cold winds. Like all clematis it is happiest with its head in the sun and its roots in the shade. It tolerates both acid and alkaline soil, but prefers it to be well drained but moisture-retentive. It climbs by means of tendrils so give it something to latch on to, such as a grid of wire or, even simpler, fix panels of large-gauge chicken wire to the fence or wall – the silver colour soon dulls down and becomes virtually invisible. It needs no pruning unless it outgrows its allotted space, though some older stems can be shortened to encourage more vigorous new growth.

## ▲ Eccremocarpus scaber

*Chilean glory vine*
SIZE AFTER ONE SEASON: 2 x 2m
  (6ft 6in x 6ft 6in)
ULTIMATE SIZE: 3 x 5m (10 x 16ft)
This striking climber has masses of small orange-red tubular flowers from early summer to autumn, as well as attractive mid-green leaves. In warm sheltered gardens it is evergreen, and is what known as 'root hardy'. This means that if the top growth does get killed by frost, as it usually does, it will almost always produce new growth from below the soil next spring. If it does survive, it is best cut hard back in spring anyway, because it will be looking rather battered after the winter. It likes a moderately free-draining soil and a sunny position. As a rambler it needs either trellis or wire to support it against a wall or fence, or you can leave it to scramble through a large dull shrub.

## ▲ Humulus lupulus 'Aureus'

*Golden hop*
SIZE AFTER ONE SEASON: 2.5 x 2.5m (8 x 8ft)
ULTIMATE SIZE: 6 x 6m (20 x 20ft)
This perennial climber has large three-lobed leaves, which are golden in full sun or light shade, and lime green in deeper shade. In late summer it also produces clusters of hops. It dies back every autumn, when it should be cut back to within 25cm (10in) of the ground. In spring, before new growth starts in earnest, cut it right back to ground level to encourage plenty of fresh new growth. As a twiner, it needs easily accessible wires on a fence or wall to get it started, or chicken wire (see *Clematis armandii* above). The golden hop is a tolerant plant and copes with sun or shade, and most soil types. Its golden colour makes it an excellent backdrop for blue or white flowers.

## ▲ Lonicera japonica 'Halliana'

*Japanese honeysuckle*
SIZE AFTER ONE SEASON: 2 x 2m
  (6ft 6in x 6ft 6in)
ULTIMATE SIZE: 9 x 9m (30 x 30ft)
This evergreen honeysuckle is an excellent choice, with fresh green foliage and, from early to midsummer, typical white honeysuckle flowers that fade to deep yellow, giving you the two colours on the plant at once. The flowers are also deliciously fragrant. For best results, this honeysuckle likes a rich fertile soil, but it will tolerate poorer conditions. It will grow in sun or medium shade, though light dappled shade is best of all. It can look scruffy at the end of a hard winter, but fresh new growth soon appears in spring to liven it up. It needs no regular pruning, but after about five years, take the shears to any forward-growing shoots after flowering.

## ▲ Passiflora caerulea

*Passionflower*
SIZE AFTER ONE SEASON: 2 x 2m
  (6ft 6in x 6ft 6in)
ULTIMATE SIZE: 6 x 6m (20 x 20ft)

This is a vigorous climber with attractive hand-shaped leaves and curious white, purple and blue flowers from midsummer to autumn. It also has fruit in late summer and autumn, not to be mistaken for passion fruit – though they will do you no harm, they do not taste great. It is a rambler and is best trained over wires or trellis. It loses its leaves in winter and the top growth can be killed off in very cold weather, but in most cases it will produce new growth in the spring. Where space is confined, it can be cut hard back to within 1m (3ft 3in) or so of ground level in early spring and will quickly regrow. It does best in full sun but can tolerate light shade, and can cope with all soil types except very dry or very limy ones.

## ▲ Solanum jasminoides 'Album'

*White potato vine*
SIZE AFTER ONE SEASON: 2.5 x 2.5m (8 x 8ft)
ULTIMATE SIZE: 5 x 5m (16 x 16ft)
This vigorous white-flowered relative of the potato vine is ideal for growing up and over a pergola or a tree. It has attractive mid-green leaves that are evergreen in sheltered town gardens, and clusters of small white flowers with bright yellow stamens from late spring to early autumn. It is happy in most soils, except extremely dry ones, and will grow in full sun to medium shade. It is not reliably hardy in cold or exposed gardens. It is a twiner, so give it a framework of wires or stout trellis to scramble up. On a pergola, it is best to wrap the uprights with chicken wire to give it a good start.

## SHRUBS

*Shrubs, whether they are evergreen or deciduous, are the backbone of any garden. In small spaces you need to choose those that will earn their keep either by having attractive foliage, a very long flowering period, or several seasons of interest – flowers and attractive berries in winter, perhaps, or vibrant autumn colour. Anything that flowers for two weeks and then has rather dull foliage for the rest of the season – lilac springs to mind – is best avoided. The examples I have chosen are good value, even in their first year, and will go on getting even better.*

## ▲ *Buddleja* 'Lochinch'
### Butterfly bush
SIZE AFTER ONE SEASON: 2 x 1.2m
   (6ft 6in x 4ft)
ULTIMATE SIZE: 2.5 x 3m (8 x 10ft)
An excellent shrub for impatient gardeners because it is fast growing, but can easily be kept within bounds. It has long silver leaves, and 15cm (6in) long plumes of very small honey-scented violet-blue flowers from summer to autumn. In early spring, cut back the previous year's growth to within 2.5cm (1in) or so of the main stems, not only to keep it in its allotted space, but also to encourage more and larger flowers. The family's common name is the butterfly bush because butterflies really do love it. It likes a sunny spot though it will cope with some shade and is tolerant of most soil types, except very dry or very boggy ones.

## ▲ *Buddleja fallowiana* var. *alba*
### Butterfly bush
This is also an excellent shrub with leaves that are even more silvery than those of *B.* 'Lochinch'. The white honey-scented flowers have an orange eye. It grows to a similar size and needs the same treatment as *B.* 'Lochinch'.

## ▲ *Caryopteris x clandonensis* 'Heavenly Blue'
SIZE AFTER ONE SEASON: 45 x 60cm
   (18in x 2ft)
ULTIMATE SIZE: 60 x 80cm (2ft x 2ft 8in)
This dense mound-forming shrub has clusters of small intense-blue flowers from late summer to early autumn and aromatic lance-shaped grey-green leaves. It should be cut hard back to ground level each spring. It is one of those plants that can look very scruffy in spring, but have faith. It will be transformed by the end of the summer. It likes a free-draining soil, and a sheltered sunny spot.

## ▲ *Ceratostigma willmottianum*
SIZE AFTER ONE SEASON: 45 x 45cm
   (18 x 18in)
ULTIMATE SIZE: 1 x 1m (3ft 3in x 3ft 3in)
This is another late-flowering shrub with small rich violet-blue flowers from late summer until well into the autumn. Its small bright-green leaves take on a red flush in autumn before they fall. It does best in a deep rich soil, but will tolerate drier or wetter conditions. It needs a sunny position and to prevent it from becoming straggly it should be cut down to near ground level each spring. Grow it as a specimen shrub or in a group of three or five. It is also good in a container.

## ▲ *Ceanothus* 'Puget Blue'
### Californian lilac
SIZE AFTER ONE SEASON: 1.5 x 1.2m (5 x 4ft)
ULTIMATE SIZE: 3 x 3m (10 x 10ft)
A good structural evergreen shrub with dark green leaves, it is smothered in rich blue flowers in late spring to early summer. It prefers full sun but will tolerate light shade and needs a deep rich soil to do well. It dislikes poor alkaline soil. For additional enjoyment, grow a late-flowering clematis such as *C.* 'Alba Luxurians' or *C. viticella* 'Purpurea Plena Elegans' through it. After flowering, you can trim back the wood that has borne flowers, but it does not respond well to hard pruning. Ceanothus tends not to be long-lived, often dying after about ten years.

## ▲ *Cornus alba* 'Elegantissima'
### Dogwood
SIZE AFTER ONE SEASON: 1.5 x 1.2m (5 x 4ft)
ULTIMATE SIZE: 3 x 4 m (10 x 13ft)
Dogwoods are useful shrubs for small gardens since they have more than one season of interest and can easily be kept in check. They are grown primarily for their winter bark, which in this case is rich ruby-red. In spring and summer it has pale green-and-white variegated leaves, which make it a very good background plant for other shrubs or perennials, or even a host for a small-flowered clematis. Since the brightest coloured bark is produced by the previous summer's new growth, cut it

hard back to about 15cm (6in) from the ground every spring. This also encourages larger, more strikingly variegated leaves as well as restricting the shrub's overall size. It does well on all soils, including boggy ones, and will cope with full sun to medium shade.

## ▲ *Fuchsia magellannica* 'Alba'
SIZE AFTER ONE SEASON: 60 x 60cm (2 x 2ft)
ULTIMATE SIZE: 1.2 x 1.5m (4 x 5ft)
Unlike its large-flowered hybrid relatives, this fuchsia is hardy, and instead of their brightly coloured big frilly flowers, it has masses of very small simple flowers of blush-white right through the summer. It makes an attractive arching shrub and is best cut back in spring to encourage lots of fresh growth. It needs a well-drained soil and though it will tolerate a degree of shade, it does best in full sun.

## ▲ *Hebe* 'Pewter Dome'
SIZE AFTER ONE SEASON: 25 x 40cm
   (10 x 16in)
ULTIMATE SIZE: 45 x 60cm (18in x 2ft)
This hebe forms a neat dome of grey green foliage with small spikes of white flowers in late spring and early summer. The fact that it is evergreen makes it a valuable structural shrub for the winter. It does best in a well-drained, not too fertile soil and prefers sun, though it will cope with part-shade.

## ▲ *Lavandula angustifolia* 'Hidcote'
### Lavender
SIZE AFTER ONE SEASON: 30 x 45cm
   (1ft x 18in)
ULTIMATE SIZE: 45 x 50cm (18 x 20in)
This neat lavender, with thick spikes of very fragrant lavender blue flowers in summer and grey-green evergreen leaves, makes a very good edging, hedge or even block of planting in a simple formal garden. It is best to clip it over lightly once flowering has finished to remove the dead flower spikes and then again in spring, just taking off the tips of the new foliage growth to keep the plant compact and bushy. It likes to be in free-draining soil and full sun.

## ★ Lavatera 'Barnsley'

*Shrubby mallow*

SIZE AFTER ONE SEASON: 1 x 1m (5 x 3ft 3in)

ULTIMATE SIZE: 2 x 2m (6ft 6in x 6ft 6in)

This shrub is an excellent temporary space-filler, producing masses of open white flowers with a red eye from early summer to the first frosts. It also has grey-green medium-sized leaves, which are a good foil for the showier flowers. Lavatera is best cut back in the spring, removing all the wood that carried flowers the previous summer, to keep it in check and to encourage better flowering. After a few years, though, it has a tendency to sprawl untidily, so take it out.

## ★ Lavatera 'Rosea'

*Shrubby mallow*

This member of the family has soft pink flowers and is very similar in habit to *L.* 'Barnsley' (see above), though perhaps slightly bigger.

## ▲ Salix exigua

*Coyote willow*

SIZE AFTER ONE SEASON: 1.5 x 1.2m (5 x 4ft)

ULTIMATE SIZE: 4 x 5m (13 x 16ft)

This willow has beautiful, slender, bright silver leaves that respond to the slightest breeze, and is one of the few silver-leaved plants that can tolerate very wet soil. It grows well in full sun to medium shade, and is best pruned hard back in late winter every three or four years to encourage the brightest young foliage. You will lose the pale yellow catkins that year but the new foliage will more than compensate.

## ▲ Sambucus racemosa 'Sutherland's Gold'

*Golden cut-leaved elder*

SIZE AFTER ONE SEASON: 1.5 x 1.2m (5 x 4ft)

ULTIMATE SIZE: 3 x 3m (10 x 10ft)

This is a stunning foliage shrub with bright golden-yellow finely cut leaves, and like all such shrubs, produces its best display on the current year's wood, so needs to be cut back hard each spring. If left unpruned the leaves become smaller, less finely cut and a duller yellow. It tolerates all soil

types including very boggy ones and this variety is best grown in light shade, though it tolerates more sun than other golden-leaved types, which are prone to scorching.

## ▲ Santolina pinnata 'Edward Bowles'

*Cotton lavender*

SIZE AFTER ONE SEASON: 45 x 45cm (18 x 18in)

ULTIMATE SIZE: 75cm x 1m (2ft 6in x 3ft 3in)

Unlike most forms of cotton lavender, which have bright-yellow pompon-like flowers that to some minds clash rather with the grey foliage, this one has soft cream flowers. It has very small feathery leaves that are evergreen but can look a bit tired and scruffy by the spring, so a light trim with the shears just as the new growth starts will encourage it to fill out. As a Mediterranean plant, it likes free-draining soil and full sun.

# HERBACEOUS PERENNIALS

*Many herbaceous perennials, especially those that flower in late summer and early autumn, give a good show in their first season, so although most go on to give an even better show in the second and third year, they qualify as Fast Plants. For immediate impact, it is better in almost every case to grow three, five or, if space allows, seven plants of the same type in a group.*

## ▲ Achillea 'Terracotta'

SIZE AFTER ONE SEASON: 60 x 30cm (2 x 1ft)

ULTIMATE SIZE: 60 x 60cm (2 x 2ft)

This variety has flat flower heads of light brick red for a couple of months in summer, but other varieties with flowers in various shades of yellow, salmon, pink and red are also well worth considering. They all have attractive green fern-like foliage. The white achillea, *A. ptarmica* The Pearl Group has small button-like

flowers and spreads quickly, which in ideal conditions can eventually be a problem. Achilleas are tolerant of most soil conditions, though they're likely to rot in heavy wet soils in winter, and prefer a sunny position.

## ▲ Artemisia absinthium 'Lambrook Silver'

SIZE AFTER ONE SEASON: 45 x 45cm (18 x 18in)

ULTIMATE SIZE: 60 x 60cm (2 x 2ft)

This is a superb foliage plant for a sunny border. With its very finely divided bright silver foliage it is an ideal foil both for soft pastels and for 'hot' reds. Unlike other artemisias, which have rather dirty yellow flowers that are best cut off when the buds appear, this has tiny grey flowers that you do not really notice. It likes a well-drained but not dry soil and full sun. If you cut it back hard in spring, you will be rewarded with new, even brighter silver foliage.

## ▲ Aster x frikartii 'Mönch'

SIZE AFTER ONE SEASON: 45 x 30cm (18in x 1ft)

ULTIMATE SIZE: 70 x 40cm (2ft 4in x 16in)

This is the easiest Michaelmas daisy of all, with delightful lavender-blue flowers with gold centres from late summer until well into the autumn. Unlike many Michaelmas daisies, it does not suffer from mildew and has strong stiff stems so is not inclined to flop. It likes a well-drained, moderately fertile soil in full sun.

## ★ Crambe cordifolia

SIZE AFTER ONE SEASON: 1.8 x 1m (6 x 3ft 3in)

ULTIMATE SIZE: 2.5 x 1.5m (8 x 5ft)

Another huge dramatic plant, which produces a massive cloud of tiny fragrant white flowers from a clump of large architectural deep green leaves. Bees love it. It is best as a temporary plant in a small border, though lovely with roses where there is more space.

## ★ Cynara cardunculus

*Cardoon*

SIZE AFTER ONE SEASON: 2.5 x 1.2 m
 (8 x 4ft)

This relative of the artichoke makes a dramatic temporary miniature tree substitute, with huge jagged silver leaves up to 60cm (2ft) long and vivid purple thistle flowers in summer, about the size of a grapefruit. It dies down in autumn, but will produce fresh growth the following spring. Since it takes up a lot of room, in a small space it is probably most useful as a one-season wonder. It prefers a sunny position and fertile well-drained soil, and because of its height, it needs shelter from strong winds.

## ▲ Filipendula rubra 'Venusta'

SIZE AFTER ONE SEASON: 1.5 x 1m
 (5 x 3 ft 3in)

ULTIMATE SIZE: 2.5 x 4m (8 x 13ft)

This perennial produces fluffy rose-pink flowers that pale as they age above mounds of striking, large, jagged light green leaves. It does best in a sunny position, though it will tolerate some shade, and likes a moist, even boggy soil. It also looks very good by water.

## ▲ Knautia macedonica

*Red scabious*

SIZE AFTER ONE SEASON: 45 x 30cm
 (18in x 1ft)

ULTIMATE SIZE: 60 x 45cm (2ft x 18in)

This plant, with its wine-red clover-like flowers, is very fashionable and deservedly so because it flowers for months in the summer. To keep it a good compact shape, grow it in well-drained not too fertile soil and in full sun.

## ▲ Macleaya cordata

*Plume poppy*

SIZE AFTER ONE SEASON: 1.8m x 60cm
 (6 x 2ft)

ULTIMATE SIZE: 2.5 x 1m (8 x 3ft 3in)

This is great for the back of a border because it is open and airy and responds to the slightest breeze. It has tall plumes of small buff-white flowers from mid to late summer, but is worth having for its

attractive large-lobed grey-green leaves alone. It prefers sun and a moist but free-draining soil, though it will tolerate some shade and other types of soil.

## ▲ Penstemon 'Stapleford Gem'

SIZE AFTER ONE SEASON: 45 x 30cm
 (18in x 1ft)

ULTIMATE SIZE: 60 x 45cm (2ft x 18in)

This is one of the hardiest penstemons, with purple-red and pale violet foxglove-like flowers from early summer to autumn. There are many different varieties available, in colours ranging from deep wine-red through pinks and white to blue. All are just as long flowering, but some are not reliably hardy and may need winter protection. They prefer well-drained fertile soil and either full sun or part-shade.

## ▲ Perovskia 'Blue Spire'

*Russian sage*

SIZE AFTER ONE SEASON: 1m x 45cm
 (3ft 3in x 18in)

ULTIMATE SIZE: 1.2m x 60cm (4 x 2ft)

This is a striking light and airy plant with silver-grey leaves and almost white powdery stems with masses of small lavender-blue flowers from midsummer to autumn. Although it is not evergreen, its tall wiry stems give structure in the winter, so leave it until new growth starts in the spring before you cut it back to ground level. It likes free-draining rather poor soil, and full sun.

## ▲ Phlomis russeliana

SIZE AFTER ONE SEASON: 60 x 90cm (2 x 3ft)

ULTIMATE SIZE: 1 x 1.2m (3ft 3in x 4ft)

This evergreen produces large clumps of big hairy sage-green leaves, which are marvellous for suppressing weeds. In early summer it throws up tall spikes with whorls of pale sulphur-yellow flowers at regular intervals. They fade to a rich russet-brown and are well worth leaving on the plant to add structure and interest to the border in the winter months. Cut them down when new growth starts in spring. It likes a reasonably free-draining soil, and sun or part-shade.

## ▲ Rheum palmatum

*Chinese rhubarb*

SIZE AFTER ONE SEASON: 1 x 1.2m
 (3ft 3in x 4ft)

ULTIMATE SIZE: 2 x 2m (6ft 6in x 6ft 6in)

This ornamental rhubarb has huge lobed green leaves up to 90cm (3ft) long and, in early summer, tall spikes of creamy pink to red flowers, up to 2m (6ft 6in) high in its second and subsequent seasons. They turn a rich coppery brown as they die and are worth leaving on the plant. Its slightly smaller cousin *R.* 'Ace of Hearts' has red-veined leaves and pale pink flowers. Both like sun or part shade and do best in a rich, fertile, and moist soil – the more sun they get the moister the soil needs to be.

## ▲ Rudbeckia fulgida var. deamii

*Black-eyed Susan*

SIZE AFTER ONE SEASON: 60 x 30cm (2 x 1ft)

ULTIMATE SIZE: 70 x 45cm (2ft 4in x 18in)

A valuable plant for late summer and autumn colour, this has large daisy-like flowers in deep yellow with dark brown centres. It is stunning grown with the lavender-blue *Aster* x *frikartii* 'Mönch'. It does best in moist but not boggy soil, although this particular variety is more drought-tolerant than most. It likes full sun but performs well enough in part-shade.

## ▲ Verbena bonariensis

SIZE AFTER ONE SEASON: 1. 5m x 20cm
 (5ft x 8in)

ULTIMATE SIZE: 1.8 x 30cm (6ft x 12in)

This tall slender plant carries small heads of intense violet flowers on stiff, very narrow stems, making it a plant you can use at the front of the border as well as the back. It flowers right through the summer, and its russet-brown seedheads are worth leaving for winter interest. It self-seeds, but not excessively. It likes sun or part-shade and a reasonably free-draining soil.

## GROUND-COVER PLANTS

*These are plants that spread quickly horizontally to cover the soil, which not only gives a new garden a mature look, but also helps suppress weeds and so reduce the amount of maintenance needed. They are best planted in groups of three, five or seven, depending on how much space there is. They will soon knit together to form an impenetrable carpet.*

### ▲ *Campanula poscharskyana* 'E.H. Frost'

Size and spread after one season: 15 x 40cm (6 x 16in)

Ultimate size: 20cm x 1m (8in x 3ft 3in)
This plant forms central mounds of fresh green leaves from which long growths are produced that cover the ground very quickly but give it a reputation for invasiveness. While that reputation is deserved, it is very easily controlled by simply pulling off the growth by the handful when it has gone too far. This detaches, leaving the central mounds intact. Unlike the plain variety, which has starry mauve-blue flowers, the flowers of 'E.H. Frost' are ice-blue. It is also less invasive than the type. It grows in sun or part-shade, and in most soil types except very boggy ones. It will also grow in cracks in paving or walls.

### ▲ *Galium odoratum*

*Woodruff*

Size after one season: 15 x 45cm (6 x 18in)

Ultimate size: 15cm x indefinite (6in x indefinite)
This excellent ground-cover plant grows very quickly sideways rather than up, soon forming a carpet of pretty fresh green lobed leaves. It is usually deciduous, but in my own garden it keeps its leaves all winter. In late spring and early summer it has scented white starry flowers. It will carry on spreading, so either give it plenty of room or chop it back with a spade when it over-reaches itself. As a woodland plant it likes moist soil and dappled shade.

It is good used formally, in a circular brick-edged bed for instance, or informally as weed-suppressing ground cover under shrubs or trees.

### ▲ *Geranium macrorrhizum*

Size after one season: 25 x 30cm (10 x 12in)

Ultimate size: 20cm x 1.2m (8in x 4ft)
This evergreen member of the hardy geranium family is excellent in that most difficult of situations – dry shade under trees. It has attractive scalloped leaves, which have a musky scent when rubbed, and which often take on a reddish tint in autumn. In late spring it produces sprays of small flowers in either magenta (*G. m.* 'Bevan's Variety'), pink (*G. m.* 'Ingwersen's Variety') or blush white (*G. m.* 'Album'), depending on the variety. They will thrive in most soil and can cope with conditions from sun to full shade.

## GRASSES

*This is a brilliant group of plants for the impatient gardener because they grow very quickly but, except in a few cases, are not invasive. Whether deciduous or evergreen, they have a very long season of interest. Even the dead stems of deciduous grasses look great in winter. They are also good in containers.*

### ▲ *Calamagrostis* x *acutiflora* 'Karl Foerster'

Size after one season: 1.8m x 30cm (6 x 1ft)

Ultimate size: 1.8m x 60cm (6 x 2ft)
This very upright grass with fine mid-green leaves is excellent for providing height without bulk. In early summer it has brownish-pink flowers that gradually fade to buff. The dead stems and foliage turn an attractive pale gold and give valuable structure through the winter. They look marvellous with the frost on them, illuminated by the low winter sun. Cut back the dead growth as soon as new shoots start appearing in early spring.

### ▲ *Miscanthus sinensis* 'Silberfeder'

Size after one season: 2m x 30cm (6ft 6in x 1ft)

Ultimate size: 2.5 x 1.2m (8 x 4ft)
An attractive grass with slender arching mid-green leaves, this produces upright silvery flower heads in late summer/early autumn, which stay on the plant through the winter and add valuable structure to the garden. Cut all the dead growth down in early spring. *Miscanthus* prefers sun and a moist but free-draining soil. It can cope with drier soil but does not thrive when it is too wet.

### ▲ *Miscanthus sinensis* 'Malepartus'

This is similar to *M. s.* 'Silberfeder' (see above) except that its flower spikes are a rich russet-red, fading to golden-brown in autumn, and it is slightly faster to get established.

### ▲ *Molinia caerulea* subsp. *arundinacea* 'Windspiel'

Size after one season: 1.8m x 20cm (5ft x 8in)

Ultimate size: 2.5m x 30cm (8 x 1ft)
Another perennial tall slender grass with mid-green leaves, this has angular purplish-brown flower spikes from early summer, which turn golden-beige in autumn. Its name translated means 'Windplay', and certainly the flower heads dance in the slightest breeze. It likes moist but free-draining soil and either sun or part-shade.

### ▲ *Stipa arundinacea*

Size after one season: 60 x 60cm (2 x 2ft)

Ultimate size: 1 x 1.2m (3ft 3in x 4ft)
This is a very striking evergreen grass that makes a fountain of orange-streaked bright green leaves, with clouds of fine coppery seed heads from midsummer to early autumn. It colours best in a sunny position but will do well in shade. It is happy in most soils except heavy wet ones. It is also superb in a large pot as a focal point.

## BULBS

*Bulbs are great for impatient gardeners because you can buy many of them in flower in pots and can see immediately what you are getting. Remove the clump carefully from its pot and plant it in the ground or in a decorative container, or simply bury the pot and then, once the flowering is over, plant the bulbs in the soil. Or, if you can curb your impatience a little, plant spring-flowering bulbs in autumn for a great show a few months later. Spring flowering bulbs are ideal where space is limited because once they have given their show and the leaves have been allowed to die down naturally (they need to be left to do this because they are making the food for next year's flowers), they then disappear from view, leaving room for summer plants.*

### ▲ *Allium christophii*

Size after one season: 60 x 15cm (2ft x 6in)
Ultimate size: 60 x 15cm (2ft x 6in)
Alliums are very fashionable at the moment and they certainly add drama to any border. This particular variety produces long slender stems supporting large heads the size of a grapefruit in late spring and early summer. The heads are made up of masses of small, silvery-mauve star-like flowers. Once the flowers die, the heads fade to a soft biscuit colour. They are very attractive still, so are well worth leaving on the plant until they crumble. These alliums need a reasonably free-draining soil and a sunny position. They take up very little ground space, so are ideal for growing among other plants.

### ▲ *Anemone blanda* 'White Splendour'

Size after one season: 15 x 15cm (6 x 6in)
Technically this is a tuber rather than a bulb. It produces spreading mounds of fresh green divided foliage above which the large white daisy-like flowers appear in mid-spring. Where conditions are right, it quickly spreads to form a dense carpet,

which dies away in early summer and returns the following spring.

### ▲ *Iris reticulata*

Size after one season: 10–15 x 5cm (4–6 x 2in)
This is a very attractive miniature iris with deep blue velvety flowers with a splash of gold on each petal. It can start flowering as early as January. It looks terrific growing through low, ground-cover plants such as epimedium or evergreen vinca. It is also very attractive *en masse* in pots.

### ▲ *Narcissus* 'Hawera'

Size in one season: 25 x 7.5cm (10 x 3in)
There are many superb dwarf daffodils suitable for small gardens or containers, but this is one of my favourites, producing nodding clusters of canary-yellow flowers in late spring. Plant *en masse* for the best effect and leave the foliage to die down for six weeks after flowering is over, so that it can manufacture food for the bulb to produce the next year's flowers. Planting these daffodils under deciduous shrubs or among perennials will hide the dying foliage or at least distract your eye.

## ANNUALS

*Annuals grow, flower, set seed and die in one season and so are great for quick and easy colour in a new garden, or in existing borders that are lacking cohesion. Hardy annuals, which are sown directly into the soil, are very easy to grow and can be in flower in 10–12 weeks. You can buy half-hardy annuals as plants, but they should not go outside until all danger of frost has past.*

### ★ *Calendula* 'Indian Prince'

*Pot marigold*
Size in one season: 45–60 x 25cm (18–24in x 10in)
One of the very fastest annuals to flower from seed – about eight weeks – this is a cottage-garden favourite. This variety has deep orange flowers – very fashionable

now – and looks marvellous on its own or grown with deep blues such as love-in-a-mist or cornflowers. Its flowers are edible and add a real visual zing to any salad. It self-seeds very easily.

### ★ *Centaurea cyanus* 'Black Ball'

*Cornflower*
Size in one season: 60–90 x 20cm (2–3ft x 8in)
A modern version of the old cottage-garden favourite, this has very dark red, almost black flowers, a colour that is very fashionable now. Unlike blue cornflowers, these do not lose their colour as the flowers age.

### ★ *Eschscholzia californica*

*California poppy*
Size in one season: 25 x 20cm (10 x 8in)
A superb annual for poor dry soil or gravel in a sunny spot, it has fern-like grey leaves and papery poppy flowers in a range of colours from fiery red through to creamy white. It self-seeds freely in soil and in cracks between paving and in very mild winters a number of the plants survive. Some of the best varieties are the orange-scarlet *E. c.* 'Inferno', the vibrant *E. c.* 'Orange King' and the pale *E. c.* 'Jersey Cream'. A smaller variety is the pale yellow *E. c.* 'Moonlight'.

### ★ *Helianthus annuus*

*Sunflower*
Size in one season: 2m x 30cm (6ft 6in x 1ft)
The best fast annual there is and, grown *en masse*, it is a great and stylish space filler. As well as the classic giant yellow variety, look for the rich mahogany 'Velvet Queen', or the very pale lemon 'Italian White', both slightly smaller at around 1.5m (5ft). Sow the seeds directly in soil or in compost in a large pot in mid-spring.

### ★ *Limnanthes douglasii*

*Poached egg plant*
Size in one season: 15 x 10cm (6 x 4in)
This annual gets its common name from its small flowers that have bright yellow centres and white edging. It is very good

at the front of a border in a sunny spot, and is another self-seeder, so once you have sown it you will always have it.

### ★ *Lupinus* subsp. *cruckshanski* 'Sunrise'

*Lupin*

SIZE IN ONE SEASON: 1m x 25cm
  (3ft 3in x 10in)

This has striking spikes of blue, white and yellow flowers above clumps of blue-green foliage. Grow it in large groups for most impact. It likes average soil and sun.

### ★ *Nigella damascena* 'Miss Jekyll'

*Love-in-a-mist*

SIZE IN ONE SEASON: 45 x 15cm (18 x 6in)

This is one of the best and easiest hardy annuals with very fine feathery foliage and rich blue flowers, followed by biscuit-brown seed capsules that look like precious stones in an ornate filigree setting. It likes a sunny position. Another rampant self-seeder. It can be sown in autumn for an earlier show the following year.

### ★ *Papaver rhoeas* 'Mother of Pearl' *and* 'Angels' Choir'

*Shirley poppy*

SIZE IN ONE SEASON: 30 x 10cm
  (12 x 4in)/70–90 x 15cm
  (2ft 6in–3ft x 6in)

These mixtures both have delicate pastel flowers, ranging from white and pale pink through peach, soft blue, lavender or even grey. Save seedheads of the colours you particularly like for sowing the following year. Poppies prefer well-drained soil and sun.

## EDIBLE ORNAMENTALS

### ★ *Runner bean*

SIZE IN ONE SEASON: 2.5m (8ft)

This attractive annual climber has bright red flowers and light green leaves and of course, an edible bonus. Grow them from seed in early spring or as young plants a few weeks later, either up a fence – attach chicken wire to it to provide support – or on a wigwam.

### ★ *Courgette*

SIZE IN ONE SEASON: 45 x 80cm
  (18in x 2ft 8in)

These make great space-fillers in a new garden, with large architectural leaves, bright orange flowers (which are edible) and the bonus of the courgettes. You can also grow them in rich compost in large containers.

## THE UNGOVERNABLE – FAST PLANTS TO AVOID

*These are plants, which although undeniably fast, just don't know when to stop, and very quickly create problems as you try to keep them in check.*

*Akebia quinata*

x *Cupressocyparis leylandii* (Leyland cypress)

*Fallopia baldschuanica* (Russian vine or mile-a-minute)

*Lamium galeobdolon* (dead nettle)

*Miscanthus sacchariflorus*

*Rosa filipes* 'Kiftsgate'

*Sedum acre* (stone crop)

## medium plants

These are plants that will give some sort of show in the first season but will really come into their own in their second and third season. Again, their size depends to some extent on the size they were when planted, but this is less of a factor than with Fast Plants.

## CLIMBERS/WALL SHRUBS

There are many different sorts of clematis that can be categorised as Medium Plants, but I have selected those that are easiest to grow. All of these like the same conditions – rich, moist but not boggy soil, with their heads in the sun and their roots in the shade. I have also selected a number of other climbers that can be categorised as Medium Plants.

### Clematis alpina 'Frances Rives'
Size after 2/3 seasons: 2 x 1.5m (6ft 6in x 5ft)
Ultimate size: 3 x 2m (10 x 6ft 6in)
This is a delightful spring-flowering clematis with nodding bell-shaped flowers that are rich blue on the outside and white in the centre. It has bright green fern-like foliage. It does not need much pruning – remove any dead or damaged stems and, if it outgrows its allotted space, cut it back once flowering is finished. It's a good climber to grow through large shrubs or roses.

### Clematis 'Bill MacKenzie'
Size after 2/3 seasons: 5 x 2m (16ft x 6ft 6in)
Ultimate size: 7 x 3m (23 x 10ft)
This is a much more vigorous clematis, with masses of small, open, bell-shaped bright yellow flowers from midsummer onwards. As they fade they turn into silvery fluffy seedheads, so you get the two colours on the plant at the same time. If left unpruned, it can become very tangled

Virginia creeper (*Parthenocissus henryana*)

and woody, so cut it back by about two thirds in the spring, and it will rapidly regrow during the summer to flower well again.

## Clematis macropetala 'Markham's Pink'

SIZE AFTER 2/3 SEASONS: 2 x 1.5m (6ft 6in x 5ft)

ULTIMATE SIZE: 3 x 2m (10ft x 6ft 6in)
This is very similar in flowers and flowering time to *C. alpina*. This variety is sugar pink, though there are others that are blue and white, or white. It needs similar conditions and treatment to *C. alpina*.

## Clematis 'Gravetye Beauty'

SIZE AFTER 2/3 SEASONS: 2.5 x 1m (8ft x 3ft 3in)

ULTIMATE SIZE: 2.5 x 1m (8ft x 3ft 3in)
Another late-flowering clematis, this time with nodding tulip-like flowers in rich ruby-red. When it is happy, it is very free-flowering indeed. Treat it as you would *C. viticella* (see below).

## Clematis viticella 'Purpurea Plena Elegans'

SIZE AFTER 2/3 SEASONS: 3 x1m (10 x 3ft 3in)

ULTIMATE SIZE: 3 x 1m (10 x 3ft)
This is a beautiful clematis with small frilly pompon flowers, the texture of faded velvet, in a rich purple. It flowers from midsummer through to autumn. There are other good clematis viticella hybrids, such as the white *C. v.* 'Alba Luxurians', pale lilac 'Betty Corning' and the wine-red 'Madame Julia Correvon'. The viticella hybrids are very easy to prune. In early spring, you simply cut them down to the first pair of fat buds, about 15cm (6in) above the ground, and they will make the same amount of growth during the season that follows. They are ideal for growing through spring and early summer flower shrubs, adding interest when the flowers of these have faded, and because they are cut back to ground level in spring, they do not interfere with the host plant's own flowering display.

## Cytisus battandieri

*Pineapple broom*

SIZE AFTER 2/3 SEASONS: 3.5 x 3.5m (11ft 6in x 11 ft 6in)

ULTIMATE SIZE: 7.5 x 7.5m (25 x 25ft)
In perfect growing conditions, this makes a very large shrub, and so is ideal against a high wall. In early to midsummer it has plumes of golden-yellow flowers that smell of ripe pineapple – hence its common name – and felty silver-green leaves. It doesn't respond well to having its old wood cut back, so if you need to keep it in check, prune back the new wood immediately after flowering. It likes soil that is well-drained but moist and not too fertile. It needs sun and shelter from cold winds.

## Hedera helix 'Goldheart'

*Ivy*

SIZE AFTER 2/3 SEASONS: 2.5 x 1.5m (8 x 5ft)

ULTIMATE SIZE: 7.5 x 6m (25 x 20ft)
This is an excellent climber for a shady wall or fence, because the central gold splash on its small five-pointed evergreen leaves brings its own sunshine to an otherwise gloomy area. Only the new growth is self clinging, so when you buy a plant, leave the cane in place to support the old growth until the new attaches itself to the wall. For speedier coverage, lay a couple of stems along the ground at the base of the wall or fence. They will root at each pair of leaves, and these will then produce new growths that climb upwards. It needs moist soil to thrive and will grow in anything from full sun to full shade, though the variegations will be a little less bright in shade. Prune it only to keep it in check or to remove stiff woody upright adult growth, the leaves of which look quite different to those on the young climbing stems. Any shoots that revert to plain green should be cut out as soon as they are noticed.

## Holboellia latifolia

SIZE AFTER 2/3 SEASONS: height or spread 4m (13ft)

ULTIMATE SIZE: height or spread 5m (16 ft)
This vigorous evergreen climber for a warm sunny wall is worth growing for its elegant oblong green leaves and clusters of small scented purple-flushed white flowers in spring. It does best in a moist rich soil, sheltered from cold winds, and in full sun or part-shade.

## Jasminum officinale

*Jasmine*

SIZE AFTER 2/3 SEASONS: 3.5 x 3.5m (12ft 6in x 12ft 6in)

ULTIMATE SIZE: 11 x 11m (36 x 36ft)
From midsummer to early autumn this has the most deliciously fragrant white flowers. Although it is slow in its first season, once established it can put on 3m (10ft) of growth in a season, so only plant it where it has plenty of space to spread. As it is a rather untidy grower, it is best in an informal setting – scrambling up a tree for example – rather than trained neatly over a garden arch. It likes full sun or just a little shade and can cope with all but the most exposed positions. It will grow well in most types of soil but does best in moist but well-drained soil. If it gets over-ambitious, prune it back in early spring. It is a semi-twiner and will need some form of support initially.

## Lonicera periclymenum 'Graham Thomas'

*Honeysuckle*

SIZE AFTER 2/3 SEASONS: 2 x 2m (6ft 6in x 6ft 6in)

ULTIMATE SIZE: 7 x 7m (23 x 23ft)
This variety has very fragrant yellow-and-white flowers from early summer through to autumn. Just as good, especially if grown together for the longest flowering period, are the Early Dutch, *L. p.* 'Belgica' and the Late Dutch, *L. p.* 'Serotina' which have creamy-white flowers heavily streaked with red and dark purple-red respectively. They are all twiners and so will need the support of wires or trellis. As they are woodland plants, they enjoy dappled shade

**slow plants**

## TREES

*Although from the moment you put it in, a tree will be the tallest plant in your garden, the trees I have listed here have been chosen because they are a long-term investment and will take a good few years to start looking really good. You may feel, as an impatient gardener, that you can't wait for a result, but time passes far more quickly than you think. We spent the first three years in our first garden saying there was no point in planting asparagus because it would take three years before we could really enjoy it.*

*So plant a tree for delayed gratification and look for your instant buzz from the Fast and Medium plant lists. And if, as an impatient gardener, you think there is no point in planting trees because you will probably not stay in the house long enough to get the benefit, grow a small tree in a large container so that you can take it – and its years of maturity – with you when you move. Or you could plant one in the garden as an act of generosity for the people who come after you. On the basis of what goes around comes around, you may be lucky enough to inherit your next garden from someone who has been equally altruistic. All the trees listed are suitable for small gardens, although many of them will eventually – after 25 years or so – reach 10m (33ft) or more. Not that you are likely to still be there to see it ...*

### Acer capillipes
*Snakebark maple*

Size after 5 years: 3 x 1.5m (10 x 5ft)
Ultimate size: 9 x 6m (30 x 20ft)

This tree is grown primarily for its very attractive bark in winter, which is green mottled with white veining, rather like snakeskin, and which becomes much more marked as the tree matures. Its typical maple leaves turn brilliant red in

**Chinese witch hazel (*Hamamelis* x *intermedia* 'Pallida')**

autumn. It forms a rounded tree and is an attractive shape when the branches are bare in winter. Tolerant of most soils, like all trees it needs plenty of water in its first few years.

## Acer palmatum var. dissectum

### Cut-leaved Japanese maple

SIZE AFTER 5 YEARS: 80cm x 1m
  (2ft 8in x 3ft 3in)

ULTIMATE SIZE: 1.5m x 2m (5ft x 6ft 6in)

This is a superb small tree for very small gardens, especially those with a Japanese theme, and grows well in a container, making it eminently portable. It forms a mound of delicate finely cut leaves that turn either gold or red in autumn. There are many excellent varieties – some with green leaves, others with rich purple ones, such as A. p. 'Garnet' or A. p. var. dissectum 'Crimson Queen'. Ideally it needs a position sheltered from wind, which can scorch the young leaves, and it does best in dappled shade. Avoid placing it where it gets early morning sun, since the warmth can thaw frosted growth too quickly and turn it brown. It dislikes limy soil, so if that is what you have, grow it in lime-free compost in a container.

## Amelanchier x grandiflora 'Ballerina'

### Snowy mespilus

SIZE AFTER 5 YEARS: 3 x 3m (10 x 10ft)

ULTIMATE SIZE: 6 x 6m (20 x 20ft)

Delightful as a small tree on a bare trunk or as a multi-stemmed shrub, this really earns its keep, with coppery new leaves in spring slightly before or at the same time as clusters of white flowers, and rich red and purple autumn colour. As a woodland plant, it does best in moist but well-drained lime-free soil, and in sun or part-shade. It needs no pruning, but it can be cut back after flowering if it outgrows its allotted space.

## Arbutus x andrachnoides

### Strawberry tree

SIZE AFTER 5 YEARS: 1 x 1m
  (3ft 3in x 3ft 3in)

ULTIMATE SIZE: 5 x 5m (16 x 16ft)

This makes a superb small evergreen tree with glossy green leaves, interestingly twisted branches covered in rich cinnamon-coloured peeling bark in winter, clusters of small, bell-like white flowers from autumn to spring, and round, orange-red strawberry-like fruits, which give it its common name. It does best in rich, moist but free-draining soil and, unlike some other members of the family, can tolerate lime. It prefers full sun, though it can cope with some shade, and does best when sheltered from cold winds.

## Betula jacquemontii

### Silver birch

SIZE AFTER 5 YEARS: 6 x 1.5m (20 x 5ft)

ULTIMATE SIZE: 12 x 1.5m (40 x 5ft)

Although this is a very tall tree it is slender and open in habit so it does not create a large amount of shade. It looks very good as a multi-stemmed tree or grown in a group if space allows. This variety has very bright white bark in winter, which brings welcome brightness into the garden, yellow catkins in spring and mid-green leaves that turn gold in autumn.

## Magnolia stellata

### Star magnolia

SIZE AFTER 5 YEARS: 1.2 x 1.5m (4 x 5ft)

ULTIMATE SIZE: 2.5 x 3.5m (8ft x 11ft 6in)

This delightful small magnolia has masses of large star-like flowers before its leaves appear in spring, starting usually within two years of planting. Its leaves are mid green, and it is an ideal host for late small-flowered clematis. It will tolerate most soil types, except extremely limy ones, and is best planted where it will not get early morning sun, which can damage the flowers by warming them up too quickly.

## Malus floribunda

### Japanese crab apple

SIZE AFTER 5 YEARS: 3 x 2.5m (10 x 8ft)

ULTIMATE SIZE: 7 x 8m (23 x 26ft)

On mature trees the branches reach down to the ground, creating a mound of foliage and flowers in the spring. The flowers are particularly attractive, opening from warm red buds to pink flowers, which fade to white as they age, giving three colours on the plant at once. These are followed by very small pea-like yellow fruits. The best fruiting variety is M. 'John Downie' and the best purple-leaved variety is M. 'Royalty' because it keeps it leaf colour right through the summer and has both light purple-red flowers and fruits. It will tolerate most soil types, except extremely wet or dry ones, and will cope with light shade, though it flowers best in full sun.

## Prunus x subhirtella 'Autumnalis'

### Winter-flowering cherry

SIZE AFTER 5 YEARS: 2.5 x 2m
  (8ft x 6ft 6in)

ULTIMATE SIZE: 8 x 8m (26 x 26ft)

This is an invaluable tree since it flowers when little else does – from autumn through to spring, whenever the weather is mild enough. It has clusters of semi-double blush-white flowers on bare wood and in autumn its leaves turn yellow before they fall. Its open canopy means it does not cast too much shade. It is tolerant of most soils, but struggles on very thin poor soil. It takes a few years to get going, but is well worth the wait.

## Prunus 'Taihaku'

### Great white flowering cherry

SIZE AFTER 5 YEARS: 3.5 x 2.5m
  (11ft 6in x 8ft)

ULTIMATE SIZE: 8 x 9m (26 x 30ft)

A stunning sight in blossom, when its branches are covered in clusters of large single pure white flowers among new foliage that may still be tinged with copper before it assumes its usual bright light green. It will cope with most soil types except very poor ones, and does best in full sun, though it tolerates light shade well enough.

### Pyrus calleryana 'Chanticleer'

*Ornamental pear*

Size after 5 years: 3 x 2m (10 x 6ft 6in)
Ultimate size: 8 x 4m (26 x 13ft)
Though less well known than the other ornamental variety, the weeping silver-leaved pear, this is a better choice for small gardens because its slender columnar habit means that it takes up less room. It has plenty of white blossom in early spring, followed by glossy bright green leaves, which usually stay into late autumn when they turn vivid orange before falling. It will tolerate all but the poorest soil, though it does best in fertile, moist but free-draining soil and full sun.

### Sorbus vilmorinii

Size after 5 years: 2.5 x 1.5m (8 x 5ft)
Ultimate size: 5 x 4m (16 x 13ft)
One of the best small garden trees, this has very attractive fern-like leaves that have good orange and red autumn colour, as well as white flowers in late spring which are followed by bright pink berries in autumn and winter. It has an open airy habit, so casts very little shade. It is tolerant of almost all soil types and produces the best autumn foliage colour and berry colour in full sun.

### Sorbus cashmiriana

Size after 5 years: 2m x 90cm
   (6ft 6in x 3ft)
Ultimate size: 4 x 4m (13 x 13ft)
No apologies for including another sorbus. This is even smaller than *S. vilmorinii* (see above), has very similar leaves, which turn yellow in autumn, and white flowers and pearl-white berries in autumn. It likes similar growing conditions.

## CLIMBERS

### Hedera colchica 'Dentata Variegata'

*Persian ivy*

Size after 5years: 2.2 x 2.2m (7 x 7ft)
Ultimate size: 7.5 x 7.5m (25 x 25ft)
This ivy, which has large, heart-shaped, evergreen, leathery grey-green-and-cream variegated leaves, is ideal for a large shady wall or for covering an unattractive building such as a garage or shed. It prefers light shade but will cope with deeper shade and even full sun, provided the soil is moist enough. It will tolerate almost all soil types. Only new growth is self-clinging, so existing growth will need some support when you plant it. It needs no pruning, but if it gets too big you can cut it back. The impatient gardener can plant fast-growing annual or perennial climbers with it for instant gratification, and remove them once the ivy fills out.

### Hydrangea anomala subsp. petiolaris

*Climbing hydrangea*

Size after 5 years: 1.8 x 1.8m (6 x 6ft)
Ultimate size: 12 x 12m (40 x 40ft)
This is an excellent choice for a shady wall, since it is self-clinging, and though it is not evergreen, it does offer interest all year. In spring its new leaves are a fresh light green, in early summer – once it is well established – it has masses of flat white flower heads, which fade slowly to pink and then turn rich russet-brown in autumn, as do the bare stems once the leaves have fallen. It grows well in sun or shade, and as long as it has plenty of moisture when young, will tolerate all soils.

### Trachelospermum jasminoides

*Star jasmine*

Size after 5 years: 1.5 x 1.5m (5 x 5ft)
Ultimate size: 4.5 x 4.5m (15 x 15ft)
This is a wonderful evergreen climber for a south- or south-west facing wall in a warm sheltered garden. It has attractive, glossy, elliptical evergreen leaves and small, white sweetly scented flowers in summer. It is not self-clinging so will need the support of wires or trellis or even individual lead-headed nails. It is tolerant of most soils except very dry ones and of full sun or light shade. It needs no regular pruning, except if it outgrows it allotted space. Unlike most plants, which establish better and more quickly when they are small, this seems to do better when planted as a large specimen – 2m (6ft 6in) or so.

### Wisteria floribunda

*Wisteria*

Size after 5 years: 5.5 x 5.5 m (18 x 18ft)
Ultimate size (after 50 years or more):
   15 x 15m+ (50 x 50ft+)
This is one of the most spectacular climbers with light green fern-like foliage and long tassels of scented blue-mauve flowers in mid- to late spring. Although it grows quite quickly, it is included in Slow plants because it can take five years or so to flower. If possible, buy a plant with at least one flower on it because then you will know it can do it. A few plants, particularly those grown from seed, will never flower. It is tolerant of most soil types, but must have plenty of room for its roots to spread. It does best in a sheltered position – a south- or west-facing wall for example – in full sun or light shade. To ensure free flowering it needs to be pruned twice – once in late summer when you cut back all the whippy new growth to about 30cm (1ft) and then again in winter when you reduce them to two buds from their point of origin. Old, really well-established plants can simply be trimmed with the shears in late summer.

## SHRUBS

### Buxus sempervirens 'Suffruticosa'

*Dwarf box*

Size after 5 years: 60 x 75cm
   (2 x 2ft 6in)
Ultimate size: 1 x 1.5m (3ft 3in x 5ft)
Ideal in small formal gardens as a low edging plant that responds well to clipping. It will grow in sun or shade and will tolerate all soil types, though the better the soil, the more quickly it will grow. Ordinary box, (*B. sempervirens*), is ideal for topiary shapes – spheres, cubes, obelisks, lollipops – and if you want a Fast plant, buy them ready-trained (see page 146)

## Cordyline australis

*New Zealand cabbage palm*

SIZE AFTER 5 YEARS: 1 x 1m
  (3ft 3in x 3ft 3in)

ULTIMATE SIZE: 4 x 3m (13 x 10ft)

This spiky architectural evergreen has long sword-like leaves growing initially at ground level and then, as the plant slowly matures, at the top of a slender bare trunk. Plants over five years old also produce bunches of small, white scented flowers. It makes a very good container plant, especially in colder gardens where it can be protected more easily during the winter. It likes very well-drained soil and full sun or very light shade.

## Cotoneaster dammeri

SIZE AFTER 5 YEARS: 20cm x 1m
  (8in x 3ft 3in)

ULTIMATE SIZE: 20cm x 2m (8in x 6ft 6in)

This low creeping evergreen is ideal as ground cover or for planting on slopes. It has pretty white flowers in early summer and bright red round berries in autumn. It tolerates most soils and will grow well in full sun or medium shade. It needs no pruning except when it outgrows its allotted space, but that will not be for some years.

## Daphne odora 'Aureomarginata'

SIZE AFTER 5 YEARS: 50 x 80cm
  (20in x 2ft 8in)

ULTIMATE SIZE: 1.5 x 1.5m (5 x 5ft)

This slow-growing mound-shaped shrub has deliciously scented mauve-pink flowers, often pale pink or white inside, in late winter and early spring. It has glossy green leaves narrowly edged with gold. Rich deep moist soil suits it best and it prefers light shade to full sun. It is an excellent plant for a container near a door where its fragrance can best be enjoyed.

## Euonymus fortunei 'Emerald Gaiety'

SIZE AFTER 5 YEARS: 60cm x 1m
  (2ft x 3ft 3in)

ULTIMATE SIZE: 60cm x 3m (2 x 10ft)

This tough, attractive, variegated evergreen shrub is very slow growing so is ideal for containers, window boxes or even hanging baskets in shady positions. This variety has grey-green-and-white variegated leaves, while the equally popular *E. f.* 'Emerald 'n' Gold' has bright yellow-and-green variegations, bringing its own sunshine to a shady spot. It is tolerant of all soil types and will grow in sun or shade, making it ideal for that most difficult of situations – dry shade under trees. It needs no pruning, but on mature plants removing a few of the older shoots will keep it vigorous.

## Hamamelis x intermedia 'Pallida'

*Chinese witch hazel*

SIZE AFTER 5 YEARS: 30 x 75cm
  (1ft x 2ft 6in)

ULTIMATE SIZE: 50cm x 1m (20in x 3ft 3in)

This is one of the best of the scented winter-flowering shrubs, with large spidery pale yellow flowers on bare wood from midwinter onwards. Its oval leaves turn a rich orange-yellow in autumn and in outline it is an attractive vase shape. It needs a neutral to acid soil – any lime will cause chlorosis – and does best in full sun.

## Hibiscus syriacus 'Oiseau Bleu'

SIZE AFTER 5 YEARS: 1 x 1m
  (3ft 3in x 3ft 3in)

ULTIMATE SIZE: 2.5 x 2m (8ft x 6ft 6in)

This shrub has blue trumpet flowers from late summer to mid-autumn and forms an attractive goblet-shaped plant. It needs an open free-draining soil and prefers light shade, though it will also tolerate full sun.

## Hydrangea aspera subsp. sargentiana

SIZE AFTER 5 YEARS: 1.2 x 1.2m (4 x 4ft)

ULTIMATE SIZE: 3 x 2.5m (10 x 8ft)

In addition to flat heads of violet-blue and white (or pink on limy soils) flowers from late summer to mid-autumn, this shrub has beautiful dark green leaves with the texture of velvet. It needs a moist rich soil and light to medium shade. It does not like full sun.

## Ilex aquifolium 'Golden van Tol'

*Holly*

SIZE AFTER 5 YEARS: 2 x 2m
  (6ft 6in x 6ft 6in)

ULTIMATE SIZE: 4 x 3m (13 x 10ft)

This small variety has puckered green, almost spineless leaves, broadly edged with golden-yellow. It has some bright red berries in autumn and winter, but fewer than the plain green but much larger variety *I. a.* 'J.C. van Tol'. It is tolerant of most soils and will grow in conditions from full sun to medium shade, though the variegations are brightest in full sun.

## Mahonia x media 'Charity'

SIZE AFTER 5 YEARS: 1.5 x 1m (5ft x 3ft 3in)

ULTIMATE SIZE: 5 x 2.5m (16 x 8ft)

This handsome evergreen shrub has whorls of long, jagged leathery leaves and plumes of egg-yolk yellow scented flowers from late autumn to midwinter. In the first five or so years, the dead flower heads must be carefully pruned out after flowering, along with terminal clusters of leaves on non-flowering shoots. This encourages the plant to become bushy rather than tall and gangly. It does best in moist rich slightly acid soil, but will do well on most types except very limy dry soils. It likes full sun or part-shade. It will grow in deeper shade, but becomes rather open and lax and does not flower as well.

## Pieris 'Forest Flame'

SIZE AFTER 5 YEARS: 80cm x 1m
  (2ft 8in x 3ft 3in)

ULTIMATE SIZE: 4 x 2m (13ft x 6ft 6in)

A striking evergreen shrub whose new foliage is bright scarlet fading through pink, cream and pale green to a glossy mid-green by early summer. It also has clusters of lily-of-the-valley like flowers in late spring. As a woodland plant it likes part-shade and a rich moist soil that is neutral to acid. In limy areas, grow it in lime-free compost in a container.

### Pinus mugo 'Mops'

*Dwarf mountain pine*

SIZE AFTER 5 YEARS: 60 x 75cm (2ft x 2ft 6in)

ULTIMATE SIZE: 2.2 x 2.2m (7 x 7ft)

This very attractive almost spherical dwarf conifer, ideal for an oriental-style garden, is very slow growing – about 7.5cm (3in) a year. It has long fresh green needles. It likes well-drained soil and a sunny position.

### Prunus tenella 'Fire Hill'

*Dwarf Russian almond*

SIZE AFTER 5 YEARS: 90 x 60cm (3 x 2ft)

ULTIMATE SIZE: 1.5 x 1.2m (5 x 4ft)

This is another small shrub that earns its keep, with masses of dark pink almond blossom appearing along the length of its branches in spring, at the same time as its long narrow leaves. It also has good autumn colour. It will grow in almost all soil types and in sun or part-shade.

### Rhamnus alaterna 'Argenteovariegata'

*Variegated Italian buckthorn*

SIZE AFTER 5 YEARS: 2 x 1m (6ft 6in x 3ft 3in)

ULTIMATE SIZE: 5 x 4m (16 x 13ft)

This attractive variegated evergreen has small, oval grey-green leaves, margined in creamy white. It produces small rather strange yellowish-green flowers in late spring, followed by bright red berries, but is grown primarily for its foliage. It likes well-drained soil and full sun or light shade. If plain green shoots appear, cut them out or the whole plant may revert.

### Rhododendron yakushimanum

SIZE AFTER 5 YEARS: 60 x 60cm (2 x 2ft)

ULTIMATE SIZE: 1.2 x 1.5m (4 x 5ft)

Although there are many hybrids of evergreen *R. yakushimanum*, the species is the one to grow. It is very slow-growing, forming a low mound of long, slender, leathery dark green leaves, with furry golden-brown undersides, and in late spring, masses of rose-pink buds, which open to blush-white flowers, slowly fading to white. It likes full sun or part-shade and must have lime-free soil. Its compact size

and slow-growing nature make it ideal for a container.

### Sarcococca hookeriana var. humilis

*Christmas box*

SIZE AFTER 5 YEARS: 25 x 30cm (10in x 1ft)

ULTIMATE SIZE: 60 x 90cm (2 x 3ft)

Grown primarily for its small white vanilla-scented flowers in winter, this shrub has elegant, slender evergreen leaves. Although it produces suckers, it is not invasive. It likes fertile, moist but free-draining soil and does best in full or part-shade.

### Syringa microphylla 'Superba'

*Littleleaf lilac*

SIZE AFTER 5 YEARS: 60 x 50cm (2ft x 20in)

ULTIMATE SIZE: 1.2m x 90cm (4 x 3ft)

This dwarf lilac is ideal for very small gardens and bears fragrant rose-pink flowers in late spring and early summer and intermittently until autumn. To encourage new growth on older plants, remove to ground level about a third of the branches that have borne flowers. It tolerates most soils and likes full sun or light shade.

### Viburnum x burkwoodii 'Anne Russell'

SIZE AFTER 5 YEARS: 90 x 90cm (3 x 3ft)

ULTIMATE SIZE: 2 x 1.5m (6ft 6in x 5ft)

Semi-evergreen, this compact variety produces rounded heads of very sweetly scented pale pink flowers in early spring, followed by red berries that ripen to black. It likes light shade but will grow in full sun to medium shade and tolerates most soils, except extremely wet or dry.

### Viburnum davidii

SIZE AFTER 5 YEARS: 80 x 80cm (2ft 8in x 2ft 8in)

ULTIMATE SIZE: 1.2 x 1.5m (4 x 5ft)

This is grown primarily as an evergreen foliage shrub forming a mound of deeply veined, leathery dark green leaves. Its small white flowers, which are followed by bright metallic blue berries in autumn are a bonus. It is tolerant of most soils except

extremely wet or extremely dry ones but does best in fertile, moist but free-draining soil. Part-shade suits it best, but it can tolerate full sun to medium shade.

### Viburnum plicatum 'Mariesii'

SIZE AFTER 5 YEARS: 1.2m x 90cm (4 x 3ft)

ULTIMATE SIZE: 3 x 3m (10 x 10ft)

Mature plants have an attractive habit, with layered branches that look wonderful in late spring and early summer when covered with flat heads of white flowers. Its deeply ribbed fresh green leaves are also attractive. It does best in light shade, though it will grow well enough in sun or medium shade, and it is tolerant of most soil types except extremes of wet or dry. It needs no pruning.

### Yucca filamentosa

SIZE AFTER MORE THAN 3 SEASONS: 60 x 90cm (2 x 3ft)

ULTIMATE SIZE: 1.2 x 1.5m (4 x 5ft)

One of the smaller yuccas, this is an attractive plant with curly white threads along the edges of its sword-like leaves. These leaves are less sharp than those of some other yuccas. Older plants produce tall flower spikes, up to 2m (6ft 6in) high, of creamy white bell-shaped flowers. It needs a sunny spot and a very well-drained soil. It does not need pruning but any dead leaves and faded flower spikes should be removed.

## GROUND-COVER PLANTS

### Epimedium x versicolor 'Sulphureum'

*Barrenwort*

SIZE AFTER 5 YEARS: 30 x 60cm (1 x 2ft)

ULTIMATE SIZE: 30cm x 1m (1ft x 3ft 3in)

Although this has attractive sprays of sulphur-yellow flowers in late spring, it is grown primarily for its foliage. The mid-green heart-shaped leaves on wiry stems are tinged with copper when they first unfurl. A woodland plant, it does best in moist but free-draining soil and in part-shade, though this particular variety will tolerate drier soil than most.

**instant plants**

These plants are worth buying as large mature specimens because they will establish well and give your garden instant height and drama. They can be as effective a focal point as a piece of sculpture, at far less cost, though obviously they are considerably more expensive than standard-size plants.

*Box topiary*
Box topiary is perfect for a formal garden or to give instant structure in a more informal setting.

*Hosta sieboldiana* var. *elegans* *(see page 139)*
One large plant or a matching pair make a stunning, instant feature.

*Phormium tenax (see page 137)*
*New Zealand flax*
For instant impact buy a specimen 1m (3ft 3in) high and almost as wide.

*Phyllostachys nigra (see page 137)*
*Black bamboo*
A large specimen of this bamboo makes an eye-catching focal point or screen.

*Pyracantha (see page 135)*
*Firethorn*
This useful evergreen wall shrub can be bought ready-trained flat on trellis.

*Trachelospermum jasminoides* *(see page 143)*
*Star jasmine*
A large specimen of this evergreen climber will make new growth fast

*Trachycarpus fortunei*
*Chusan palm*
A terrific plant for an exotic-looking jungle garden, this has sprays of yellow flowers in spring and huge fan-like leaves.

Black bamboo (*Phyllostachys nigra*)

keeping it going

ABOVE *Epimedium* x *versicolor* 'Sulphureum' and delicate *Adiantum venustum* make good weed-suppressing ground cover, though do make sure the ground is as weed-free as possible before you plant.

ABOVE RIGHT Planting in containers is a guaranteed way of keeping weeding to the minimum.

Unlike rooms, which once decorated and furnished more or less look after themselves, gardens need a bit of looking after. Since you are an impatient gardener, time is precious. You will want to entertain, relax or sit in your garden rather than slave away in it, so what follows is simple horticultural advice with the emphasis very firmly on reducing work and saving time.

The trick is to identify the regular routine tasks that take up most time, and either eliminate them altogether, or reduce them to a bare minimum.

## Weeding

Weeding is a case in point. Wherever there is soil, there is an opportunity for weeds to get established. As with so many things, prevention is better than cure. If you are planting from scratch, make sure the soil is dug over very thoroughly and every scrap of weed root removed. Many of the worst weeds will grow from even a millimetre of root. If you don't want to weed yourself, get an experienced gardener to do it, otherwise you are wasting your money. Time – or money – spent doing this properly now will save hours of work later.

If the problem originates in a neighbouring garden you need to create a physical barrier against the encroaching weeds. Dig a trench about 30cm (1ft) deep along the base of the fence on your side, then nail a 30cm (1ft) wide strip of thick black polythene along the bottom of the fence and push it down into the trench. This will prevent most perennial weeds from creeping under the fence and into your garden.

Once the soil is as free from perennial weeds as possible, the best way to keep them at bay in the short term and to discourage annual weeds is to mulch –

**148 / the soft touches**

cover the soil with, ideally, a 10cm (4in) layer of organic material such as compost, cocoa shells or composted bark, or an inorganic layer of gravel, stone chippings or even crushed glass. Alternatively, lay a woven membrane over the soil. If you are starting from scratch, plant through it by cutting 'X's in it, opening up the flaps to make your planting holes, and folding them back once the plants are in. If you have a planted border already, you need to cut the membrane to accommodate the plants but the more cuts you make, the more opportunity there is for the weeds to come through. Once the membrane is laid, cover it with a purely ornamental layer of gravel or bark.

Any annual weeds that germinate can't penetrate the membrane nor can the new growth of most perennial weeds, although the real thugs can almost force their way through concrete.

If you use a mulch on its own, by the time annual weed seedlings have fought their way through it to reach the light, they are so weak and spindly that they are very easily pulled out.

In the longer term, ground-cover plants are a good and attractive way of keeping weeds under control, but be warned that trying to remove established weeds from ground cover planting is a nightmare.

## Watering

Watering is another routine job that needs to be done regularly. Choosing drought-tolerant plants is sensible, but even they need regular thorough watering when first planted until they are established.

Mulching can help cut down on watering. Apply a mulch when the soil is already moist and it will help keep moisture in.

ABOVE **A very attractive, low-maintenance front garden features a combination of hard materials and low ground-cover planting.**

RIGHT The evergreen *Ceanothus* 'Puget's Blue' needs no regular pruning. All you need to do is remove any dead wood.

FAR RIGHT *Buddleja* 'Lochinch' flowers after midsummer on the current season's wood. Just cut it back to about 30cm (1ft) from the ground in late autumn or early spring.

If you really can't devote time to watering, then install an automatic watering system. The simplest consists of a soaker hose – a porous pipe that slowly seeps water along its entire length. Lay it permanently on the soil around the base of shrubs and trees and weave it in and out of the smaller plants. You can cover it with soil or with a mulch. Attach it to a water computer fixed to an outside tap.

For containers you need a micro-irrigation system, which can also be used in borders. It consists of a feeder hose into which much narrower plastic pipes are fixed. These have either a drip feeder or small spray on a spike at the other end. The spikes are then pushed into the soil and the water is delivered where it is needed. This system can also be controlled by a water computer.

Another way of reducing the amount of watering needed by containers is to mix water-retaining gel crystals into the compost as you plant. These crystals are able to hold hundreds of times their own volume of water, which they then release gradually into the compost, keeping it moist.

## Feeding

As an impatient gardener, you will want to get your plants off to a flying start, and so you will need to feed them. If you are planting from scratch, the best way of feeding, undoubtedly, is to dig in some decent organic matter such as well-rotted manure or garden compost, but only one shovelful of manure every square 1m (3ft), and two shovelfuls of garden compost. The temptation is to add a little bit extra in the hope of making your plants grow even faster, but that would be a mistake. If you do this, they will only produce plenty of soft sappy growth that is prone to all sorts of pests and diseases and which may then have to be cut out, thus defeating the object of the exercise.

If you are planting in an existing border, you can mix some manure or compost into the soil at the bottom of the planting hole and into the soil with which you refill the hole. Or you can add an organic fertilizer such as blood, fish and bone or pelletted chicken manure. If you are not concerned about being organic, you can use an inorganic fertilizer. The easiest to use are controlled-release fertilizers, which will last a whole season.

ABOVE **Small late-flowering clematis such as the viticella and texensis hybrids are the easiest to prune. Remove all dead growth in late winter, cutting just above the first pair of leaf buds on the main stems.**

These come as granules or thimble-shaped plugs, which are perfect for containers because you simply push them into the compost when you plant and then can forget about feeding until next year. You can even use them if you plant in autumn because the coating of the granules is heat-sensitive, so when the soil or compost is too cold for the plants to be growing and needing fertilizer, they do not release any nutrients. They only start to release their nutrients when the soil or compost warms up and the plants start to grow and need feeding. Again, stick to the recommended amount and don't add a bit extra just for luck.

## Pruning

Pruning is a subject that people who do not consider themselves to be gardeners find terrifying and so avoid as far as possible. Although there are thick tomes written on the subject, in fact, for the most widely grown garden plants, pruning really isn't that difficult and can be boiled down to relatively few rules of thumb.

It helps to understand why you need to prune. First of all, it keeps plants within the space allotted to them.

While you could grow only plants that will always remain very small, you will have a rather dull garden. For the sake of fifteen minutes or so once a year – all it takes to prune most plants – is it not more rewarding to grow some bigger, much more exciting specimens and keep them under control?

The second reason for pruning is to keep the plant young, healthy and vigorous by removing some of the old tired wood. Most shrubs flower more freely on younger wood and produce larger flowers, too. And if the shrubs feature coloured leaves and bark, pruning will produce bigger and more intensely coloured leaves and brighter bark.

Many new gardeners are frightened they will kill plants if they prune them incorrectly. In fact it is very hard indeed to kill a plant by pruning it. A trial was carried out at the Royal National Rose Society's gardens in the 1990s in which three beds of the same variety of rose were pruned in different ways. The first were pruned correctly with secateurs, the second were also pruned with secateurs but badly, while the third group were hacked with a hedge trimmer. Guess which roses flowered best the following year? The hedge trimmer group. The bushes themselves looked a bit of a mess after a couple of years of this treatment and so for that reason it is not a method I would recommend, but it does show that you really do not need to worry about getting it wrong.

In most cases, the worst that is likely to happen is that if you prune at the wrong time of year you will lose that season's flowers.

Most flowering shrubs and climbers such as clematis fall into two groups. The first are the spring- and early-summer flowering types – forsythia and philadelphus for example. These flower on growth they made the previous summer, therefore they need to be pruned immediately they have finished flowering so that during the rest of the summer they can produce the wood on which the next year's flowers will form. Cut back all of the growth that has borne flowers to the point from which a healthy new shoot is emerging.

The second group are those plants that flower after midsummer – buddleja for instance, or clematis viticella hybrids. These only produce flowers on growth they have made in the current season, so the old growth needs to be pruned back hard in late autumn after flowering or better still, in very early spring just as the plants start growing. If you don't prune, you will get flowers high up, on the new season's growth, and the flowers will be smaller and fewer, too.

Most roses fall into this second category, though I would recommend you avoid planting those that need extensive annual pruning – primarily the hybrid teas or floribundas. This is not just to save you time. Personally, I think these roses make very ugly plants during the winter months, and there are so many more attractive and more easily maintained types to choose from – modern shrub roses, English roses, patio roses and so on. All these need in the way of pruning is the removal of dead wood, along with any diseased or very weak and spindly growth. Keep them in check by removing 15–20cm (6–8in) of stem as you deadhead – that is, cut off dead flowers in summer to encourage the plant to produce more blooms. Cutting out an older stem or two right down to ground level in early spring every few years will keep the plant vigorous by encouraging strong new growth from the base.

Evergreens should be pruned in late spring, but only when necessary to keep them within bounds and to maintain an attractive shape. Take it slowly, a little at a time, standing back frequently and having a good look at what you have done, rather than going at it like a bull at a gate. Like hair, plant growth can be snipped off in a second but can take a long time to re-grow.

Most hedges need clipping at least twice a year to keep them looking neat. Given the time it takes, and the necessity for expensive equipment like hedge trimmers, this is a job that many impatient gardeners would rather leave to a professional.

## Propagation

Clearly, what I would not recommend for the impatient gardener is the sort of propagation that involves sowing seed, waiting four years for it to germinate and another four before the resulting seedlings are large enough to plant out. Propagation for anyone in a hurry has to be quick and easy.

Simply saving seeds from annuals such as love-in-a-mist (*Nigella*) or field poppies (*Papaver rhoeas*) is one way of increasing your stock of plants. In the case of field poppies, where the colours you get in a seed packet are mixed, saving your own seeds also allows you to choose the colours that you like best and to sow only those the following year.

Towards the end of the summer, check that the seed capsules are ripe – you can tell easily enough from the colour, which will be light or mid-brown in most cases, and from the fact that the capsule is starting to open. Shake the contents of the seed capsules into a paper (not plastic) bag, an envelope or a film container. Label them with the name of the plant and the date. A good place to store them is inside an airtight food container at the bottom of the fridge. This replicates winter and for some varieties it is essential

that they experience winter or they won't germinate in spring. Some of these annuals will germinate in autumn if, as is bound to happen, the capsules release their contents before you can collect them, but these seedlings have a higher failure rate than spring-germinating ones.

The following spring, sow your collected seeds where they are to flower. Always be very mean with them. If you sow too many, you will have to pull out most of them to leave enough room for those that remain to develop into healthy adult plants.

## Cuttings

Taking cuttings is not only an insurance policy for those plants such as rosemary that are not a hundred per cent hardy, but it is also a very good way of taking certain plants with you when you move.

Take cuttings of rosemary or lavender in summer by removing young shoots about 10–15cm (4–6in) long that have not flowered. Strip off the lower leaves, so that the bottom two thirds of the cutting is bare, and trim the base with a sharp knife just below a leaf joint. Pinch out the growing tip. Push the cuttings into a pot of moist free-draining compost, so the leaves are just clear of the surface. Then push in three short canes around the rim of the pot, and cover with a clear polythene bag, sealed underneath. This creates a moist micro-climate around the cuttings until they can put out roots to seek moisture from the soil. The canes prevent the polythene from coming into direct contact with the cuttings, which could encourage rotting.

Stand the pot on a light windowsill, but not in direct sunlight. Check it regularly, tapping the bag to make the condensation run down the sides into the compost rather than dripping on the cuttings. As soon as you can see signs of new growth, usually in three or four weeks, remove the polythene. If each cutting has plenty of space, you can leave all the cuttings in the pot until you are ready to plant them out. Otherwise, pot them on into a bigger pot. Either way, keep them in a light, cool but frost-free place until spring.

LEFT **Dense planting like this reduces the need for regular maintenance by suppressing weeds. A major annual pruning session makes sure the plants remain vigorous and yet within bounds.**

## PAINTS AND WOOD STAINS

**Multi-surface garden paint:**
B&Q Multicoat Garden
Colours. B&Q DIY and Garden
Superstores. For your nearest
branch contact B&Q on +44
(0)845 309 3099 or visit
www.diy.com
Cuprinol Multi-Surface Garden
Shades. For your nearest
stockist contact Cuprinol on
+44 (0)1753 550555 or visit
www.cuprinol.co.uk
Cuprinol Garden Shades. For
your nearest stockist see
contact details as above

**Exterior wood paint or
stain:** Dulux Aquatech in
'Pigeon'. For your nearest
stockist contact Dulux on +44
(0)1753 550555 or visit
www.dulux.co.uk

**Exterior gloss paint:** Crown
Non-drip Gloss. For your
nearest stockist contact
Crown Paints on +44 (0)1254
704951 or visit
www.crownpaint.co.uk

**Masonry paint:** Sandtex High
Cover Smooth. For your
nearest stockist contact Akzo
Nobel on +01 254 704951

**Acrylic all-surface paint:**
Plastikote. For your nearest
stockist contact Plastikote on
+44 (0)1223 8364000

## FENCING

**Large bamboo poles:** Jungle
Giants, Burford House
Gardens, Tenbury Wells,
Worcestershire WR15 8HQ

**Polypropylene rope:** B&Q DIY
and Garden Superstores. For
your nearest branch see
contact details given above

**Heather fencing:** Gardman.
For your nearest stockist
contact +44 (0)1406 372222
or visit www.gardman.co.uk

## FURNITURE

**Fibreglass chair:** Finn Stone,
25 Cumberland Road, London
N22 7TD. For details contact
Finn Stone on +44 (0)20
8889 3856 or visit
www.finnstone.com

**Softwood bench:** B&Q DIY
and Garden Superstores. For
your nearest branch see
contact details given above

## CONTAINERS

**Large 'long tom' terracotta
pots:** B&Q DIY and Garden
Superstores. For your nearest
branch contact B&Q on +44
(0)845 3093099 or visit
www.diy.com

**Versailles tubs:** Roots and
Shoots Horticultural Training
Workshop, Vauxhall Centre,
Walnut Tree Walk, London
SE11. For details contact +44
(0)20 7587 1131

**Fibreglass containers:** For
your nearest stockist contact
Evergreen Exterior Services on
+44 (0)20 8640 1000

**Galvanised metal bowl:**
Habitat Limited. For your
nearest branch see contact
details given above

**Galvanised metal containers:**
Digit.com. For details and mail
order visit www.digit.com

## ACCESSORIES

**Decorative glass marbles:**
The House of Marbles. For
your nearest stockist see
contact details given above

**Lanterns:** The Conran Shop,
81 Fulham Road, London
SW3. For details contact The
Conran Shop on +44 (0)20
7589 7401

**Crushed CDs:** Specialist
Aggregates, 162 Cannock
Road, Stafford ST17 0QJ. For
details visit www.specialistag-
gregates.com

**Plastic spirals:** Habitat
Limited. For your nearest
branch, contact +44 (0)20
7255 2525 or visit
www.habitat.co.uk

## MULCHES

**Cocoa shell mulch:** For your
nearest stockist contact
Sunshine of Africa on +44
(0)1420 511500

## ADHESIVES

**Adhesive:** Ardurit Cement-
based Adhesive. For your
nearest stockist contact Travis
Perkins on +44 (0)1604
752424 or visit
www.travisperkins.co.uk

Page numbers in *italic* refer to the illustrations

# acknowledgements

Our thanks to the owners of the gardens in which the projects were done: Isobel and Sheila de Mendoza, Caroline Williams, Lavinia Warner, Robert Stocken, Jane and Patrick O'Shea, and Graham and Isobel McCallum – for looking after the plants and making sure they thrived. Thanks, too, to The Uncommon Gardener, Jacob Papineau and his chaps who helped us with those projects that involved major construction.

We are both very grateful to Joan and Stuart Mungall of Patio, 100 Tooting Bec Road, London S.W. 18 for plants and encouragement, and to Bob and Annette Collett of Petersham Nurseries, Richmond Surrey who either sourced or grew and nurtured most of the plants for us, bringing them to their peak at exactly the right time.